AMERICAN
Holidays

Exploring
Traditions, Customs
and Backgrounds

VOCABUREADER
WORKBOOK 3

By
Barbara Klebanow
Sara Fischer, Ph.D.

Illustrated by Robert MacLean

PRO LINGUA **ASSOCIATES**

Published by Pro Lingua Associates
15 Elm Street
Brattleboro, Vermont 05301
802-257-7779
SAN 216-0579

ISBN 0-86647-018-2

This book was set in Century Oldstyle by Stevens Graphics
and printed and bound by The Book Press, both of Brattleboro,
Vermont. Designed by Arthur A. Burrows.

Printed in the United States of America.
Third printing 1990. 19,000 copies in print.

Acknowledgements

I want to thank my students at the **Great Neck Adult Learning Centers** and **North Shore Hospital** in Manhasset who over the years inspired me to write this book and who were unrelenting in their desire to learn about our American heritage.

Thanks to my parents **Mildred** and **Barnet Brodie** who came to this country almost 60 years ago fleeing religious persecution and lack of economic opportunities. Their lives demonstrated that by hard work in a sweat shop in Manhattan this is the land of opportunity. Their dreams of a better life were realized when their children became a teacher and a doctor.

Barbara Klebanow

I want to express my thanks to all the students and teachers of the **New York City** schools and the **Great Neck Adult Learning Centers** who crossed my life during the past 12 years. Their courage and dedication to learning have been inspiring and have made me proud of my profession as a teacher. I admire and respect them.

Special thanks and gratitude to this country and its people. Having come as an immigrant 20 years ago, I have known freedom and the possibility of achieving success based on my own merits. I have met with the generosity, genuine interest, and affection of dozens of people. They all helped me to learn English and to understand how people learn a new language. I am indebted to all of them.

Last, but most importantly, deep thanks to my children **Gabriel, Fabiana** and **Alejandra Lotito** without whose love, patience, humor and help I would have never been able to achieve any of my goals. They taught me about life and growing up. I love them dearly.

Dr. Sara Fischer

Special thanks are due to the **Great Neck Public Library** whose resources were always extended to us most graciously. **The New York Times** also proved to be a helpful resource.

Sara Fischer and Barbara Klebanow

I dedicate this book to Liberty's greatest symbol:

The Statue of Liberty
on her one hundredth birthday.

Barbara Klebanow

"Give me your tired, your poor,
Your huddled masses yearning to breathe free,
The wretched refuse of your teeming shore.
Send these the homeless tempest-tost to me,
I lift my lamp beside the golden door!"

Emma Lazarus

Contents

Introduction   ix

Introductory Reading   1

_ legal   _ celebrate   _ superstition
_ religious   _ commemorate   _ calendar

New Year's Days   5

_ toast   _ goal   _ ancient
_ achieve   _ prosperity   _ crowd
_ elaborate   _ embrace   _ float
_ resolution

Martin Luther King's Birthday   11

_ memorial   _ racial   _ assassin
_ clergyman   _ injustice   _ spiritual
_ segregate   _ integrate   _ discrimination
_ rights

Valentine's Day   17

_ romance   _ merchant   _ companion
_ affection   _ spouse   _ festival
_ humorous   _ feelings   _ sweetheart
_ decorate

Presidents' Day   24

- _ chop
- _ admit
- _ wrongdoing
- _ elect
- _ refuse
- _ conflict
- _ independence
- _ ideal
- _ unanimously
- _ unite

St. Patrick's Day   31

- _ celebrity
- _ bystanders
- _ participate
- _ pennant
- _ estimate
- _ capture
- _ convert
- _ miracle
- _ legend
- _ descent

Mother's Day and Father's Day   36

- _ respect
- _ raise
- _ proclaim
- _ role
- _ symbolize
- _ attend
- _ memories
- _ thoughts
- _ value
- _ establish

Memorial Day   41

- _ patriotic
- _ disabled
- _ service
- _ artificial
- _ wreck
- _ origin
- _ needy
- _ tragedy
- _ renewal
- _ benefit

Independence Day   46

- _ declare
- _ independent
- _ sworn
- _ representation
- _ obey
- _ organize
- _ naturalization
- _ force
- _ rededication
- _ recognize

Labor Day 52

_ strike
_ hire
_ wages
_ persuade
_ require
_ minimum
_ union
_ competition
_ solution
_ message

Columbus Day 57

_ contribution
_ tie
_ crude
_ encourage
_ route
_ navigate
_ finance
_ convince
_ expedition
_ comfort

Halloween 63

_ trick
_ carve
_ character
_ collect
_ evil
_ holy
_ ghost
_ costumes
_ scary
_ treat

Election Day 68

_ election
_ vote
_ duty
_ registration
_ privacy
_ advertise
_ candidate
_ result
_ campaign
_ debate

Veterans Day 73

_ remember
_ enact
_ courage
_ missing
_ observe a holiday
_ bury
_ dedicated
_ serve the country
_ honor
_ ceremony

Thanksgiving Day 78

- annual
- elderly
- feast
- harvest
- observance
- faiths
- starvation
- stuffing
- survive
- wreath

Christmas 84

- stable
- share
- sparkle
- donation
- exchange
- ornaments
- crowded
- volunteer
- display
- favorite

Birthdays 91

- represent
- wish
- appropriate
- reserve
- cater
- souvenir
- invitation
- charity
- celebration
- traditional

Appendix A:
Appropriate Gifts for Holidays 97
Appendix B: Holiday Songs 98
Appendix C: Readings for Holidays 99
Appendix D:
Holidays Around the World 102
Suggestions for the Teacher 105
Answers 110
Key Word Index 116
Bibliography 118

Introduction

American Holidays is a vocabulary development text which focuses on words which are associated with the traditions, customs, and background of the special days we celebrate in the United States. Some of these holidays are also celebrated in Canada and elsewhere. The special vocabulary is presented in seventeen readings. The reading passages are written in a redundant style so that you can learn the definition of each word through context. Although you may have to use a dictionary from time to time, you should try to understand the meaning of the word by studying the sentences which precede and follow the key word. Therefore, you can develop both new vocabulary and good reading skills. The lessons are organized according to the following plan:

Reading

Each reading selection describes an American holiday. The key vocabulary is in **bold face**. The first section of each reading explains the traditions and customs of the holiday. The second explores its historical and cultural background.

Exercises

Five or six exercises follow each reading selection. The exercises progress from easy to more difficult. In the exercises you will be required to explore the forms and meanings of the key words. The exercises are not tests. They are teaching exercises, and it is expected that you will make some mistakes. You can teach yourself by using the Answers. Sometimes the last exercise does not have answers in the book because you must create original sentences. You can use this last exercise as a test by asking someone who knows English well to check your answers.

Appendices

Each appendix contains materials for activities which supplement the readings and exercises.

Suggestion for the Teacher

Both basic techniques for using this book and ideas for supplementing it are given.

Answers

Answers for most of the exercises of each reading are found at the back of the book.

Key Word Index

This is a list of all the key words and the pages on which the lesson they appear in begins.

Introductory Reading

There are many special days in the United States; some of them are **legal** holidays. On a legal holiday, people do not go to work. Schools, businesses and government offices are closed. There are nine legal holidays that are observed throughout the country.

Some states **celebrate** local holidays to **commemorate** events that are important to that state or region. For example, on or about April 19, a famous date of the American Revolution, Massachusetts and Maine celebrate Patriots' Day. On this day, the famous race, the Boston Marathon is held.

There are also several special **religious** days. The word "holiday" is a combination of "holy" and "day," but the only religious day that is also a legal holiday is Christmas. Other well-known religious days are Good Friday and Easter (Christian) and Yom Kippur and Hannukah (Jewish).

There are three special days that are not holidays or commemorative days. One of these days is February 2nd when people in the northern part of the United States are beginning to look forward to spring. It is called Groundhog Day. There is a **superstition** that on this day a small animal, the groundhog, comes out of his hole in the ground where he has spent the winter. If the sun is shining and he sees his shadow, he will go back in his hole and there will be six more weeks of winter. If the sun is not shining, the groundhog will stay out and spring will come early.

April Fools' Day is the first day of April, a time when spring is coming and people are feeling playful. On this day people play tricks on each other. A favorite trick is to say something that is not true. If another person believes what is said, he is an "April Fool."

From time to time, Friday comes on the 13th day of the month. Friday the Thirteenth is considered an unlucky day, and some superstitious people are very careful because they are afraid that something bad may happen during the day.

The readings in this book describe the best known legal holidays and commemorative days. Use a **calendar** to fill in the month, day and date for the following holidays:

Holidays for 19____	Month	Day	Date
New Year's Day			
Martin Luther King's Birthday			
Valentine's Day			
Presidents' Day			
St. Patrick's Day			
Mother's Day			
Memorial Day			
Father's Day			
Independence Day			
Labor Day			
Columbus Day			
Halloween			
Veterans Day			
Election Day			
Thanksgiving			
Christmas			
Your Birthday			

Now learn why, where, and how Americans celebrate their holidays.

legal   **celebrate**   **superstition**
religious   **commemorate**   **calendar**

I. Use the words above to complete these sentences.

1. There are nine _____ holidays in the United States.

2. Groundhog Day is based on a _____.

3. Some states _____ their own holidays.

4. Easter is a _____ day.

5. There is a _____ on the wall.

6. Patriots' Day _____s the patriots of the American Revolution.

II. Use these forms of the key words to complete the sentences.

illegal   **religion**   **commemorative**
legally   **celebration**   **superstitious**

1. He is not scared of Friday the Thirteenth because he is not _____.

2. The government issued a _____ postage stamp for Martin Luther King, Jr.

3. In most states it is _____ to drink alcohol and drive a car at the same time.

4. In 1986 there was a great _____ for the Statue of Liberty.

5. A person without a driver's license cannot _____ drive a car.

6. Christianity is not the official _____ of the United States.

Answers are on page 110.

4

DEC. 31
OUT... ....GOES THE OLD...
New Year's Day
JAN. 1
·IN COMES THE NEW·

Traditions and Customs

New Year's Day is a popular legal holiday celebrated in the United States. The celebration begins on December 31, New Year's Eve, the night before New Year's Day. Many people stay up until midnight. Some go to church while others go to parties. Horns, whistles and other noisemakers are very popular on this night. This is an old traditon from **ancient** times when people made loud noises to scare away evil spirits.

When the ringing of bells and the blowing of whistles and horns announce that the new year has started, some people shake hands; others kiss and **embrace**.

Many join together to sing "Auld Lang Syne." In addition to blowing whistles and horns, people throw paper confetti and streamers and call out "Happy New Year," raising their drinks in a **toast** to the future, hoping it will bring health, peace, and **prosperity**.

On New Year's Eve, New York City holds an outdoor event which attracts a **crowd** of a million or more people. The event is televised around the country. A large ball shaped like an apple and covered with bright lights is slowly lowered from a pole on top of a tall building in Times Square. It starts coming down one minute before midnight. When it reaches the bottom of the pole, the new year has begun.

New Year's Day is celebrated in different ways. Many people hold "Open House," serving refreshments to visitors. Egg nog, a drink made with milk and eggs is especially popular. Others watch the parades and football games that are very typical for this day. The Mummer's Parade in Philadelphia has marchers in **elaborate** costumes. The Tournament of Roses parade in Pasadena, California is known for its **floats** decorated with fresh flowers. The most famous college football game, the Rose Bowl, is played after the parade.

Background

New Year's Day celebrates the start of a new year. People who follow the Roman calendar celebrate this holiday on January first. This month was named for Janus, the ancient Roman god with two faces, one looking into the past, the other looking into the future.

On New Year's Day people often think about the past year. They remember the projects they finished and the **goals** they did not **achieve**. Like Janus, they also look forward to a new beginning and make "new year **resolutions**" on what they will achieve.

I. Match each word with its meaning.

1. **toast**	____	**a.** many people
2. **achieve**	____	**b.** detailed; complicated
3. **elaborate**	____	**c.** to do successfully
4. **resolution**	____	**d.** decorated vehicle
5. **goal**	____	**e.** very old
6. **prosperity**	____	**f.** something to work for
7. **embrace**	____	**g.** to make a decision
8. **ancient**	____	**h.** an expression of affection; a hug
9. **crowd**	____	**i.** good fortune; success
10. **float**	____	**j.** a drink to honor something or someone

II. Select the correct choice to complete each sentence.

1. Football games attract a large (crowd, parade, toast).
2. Some marchers in the parade wear (hats, toast, elaborate) costumes.
3. The (crowds, floats, people) in the "Tournament of Roses" parade are covered with fresh flowers.
4. Making loud noises on New Year's Eve is a tradition that began in (ancient, modern, cold) times.
5. We all hope to (goal, achieve, decorate) peace in the coming year.
6. People set up new (crowds, goals, prosperity) each new year.
7. At midnight people kiss and (achieve, sit, embrace) one another.

7

8. Most people make (resolutions, parties, embraces,) that are difficult to keep.

9. Everybody hopes that the new year brings (prosperity, tradition, goals) and health.

10. When the new year arrives, many people raise their glasses and (achieve, toast, resolve) to the future.

III. Complete the following passage.

Everybody expects large _____ in Times Square on New Year's Eve. When the apple reaches the bottom of the pole, people shout "Happy New Year" and _____ one another. At the same time, people at parties blow whistles and horns, following an _____ tradition. They _____ with champagne and make personal _____ for the new year. They set up _____ to improve their life and hope they can keep them. Everyone looks to the future for peace and _____. The following day many families watch parades. They enjoy the _____ covered with flowers and the marchers in _____ costumes.

8

IV. Select words to complete these sentences.

1. The wedding celebration started with a _____ for the newly married couple.

2. The young couple worked hard so they could enjoy _____ in later years

3. The Pyramids and the Sphinx are monuments of _____ Egypt.

4. The athlete achieved her _____ when she won an Olympic gold medal.

5. The oriental rug was decorated with an _____ design.

6. The rock concert attracted a noisy _____ .

7. Musicians practice long hours to _____ their artistic goals.

8. Both friends _____ with emotion after the long absence.

9. The sisters promised to tell each other their new year _____ .

10. The students worked many hours to finish the _____ for the college parade.

9

V. Write questions that can be answered by each statement below. The first word of each question has been written for you.

Example:
New Year's Day is a legal holiday.
a. What _____

1. The New Year's holiday begins on the evening of December 31st.
   a. What _____ ?
   b. When _____ ?

2. Large crowds attend the outdoor event in Times Square, New York City.
   a. Who _____ ?
   b. Where _____ ?

3. Americans go to parties to celebrate the new year.
   a. Who _____ ?
   b. Where _____ ?
   c. Why _____ ?

4. Alfredo made a new year resolution during the New Year's holiday.
   a. Who _____ ?
   b. What _____ ?
   c. When _____ ?

5. In ancient times people made loud noises to scare away evil spirits.
   a. Who _____ ?
   b. What _____ ?
   c. Why _____ ?

Traditions and Customs

On January 15th, people in the United States cele-brate the birthday of Martin Luther King, Jr. He was a great civil **rights** leader who fought against **racial discrimination**. He said that people should be judged by their character, and not the color of their skin. He believed in **integration**. He received national attention when he protested the **injustice** of **segregated** buses in Alabama.

Martin Luther King is remembered in church **memorial** services, marches, and public ceremonies. People also listen to his speeches, watch TV documen-taries, and sing **spirituals** and the civil rights anthem

11

"We Shall Overcome." In schools, students read about this leader, study his writings and celebrate his memory with special programs. Politicians and performers also participate in celebrations to honor Martin Luther King.

The third Monday in January is a legal holiday to honor Martin Luther King.

Background

Martin Luther King, Jr., was born in Atlanta, Georgia, on January 15th, 1929. His father was a **clergyman**, Reverend Martin Luther King, Sr., and his mother was Alberta Williams King.

Martin Luther King, Jr., was an excellent student. He entered college at the age of 15 years. He was interested in history, literature, sociology and public speaking. He studied black history, religion and theology. He received his doctor of philosophy degree from Boston University.

He became a minister and married Coretta Scott. They had four children. He was the pastor of the Dexter Avenue Baptist Church in Montgomery, Alabama. Martin Luther King worked to end segregation of black people. He also became a leader of the human rights movement.

He believed in non-violent methods. In 1963, he gave one of his most famous speeches, "I Have a Dream," in front of the Lincoln Memorial, in Washington, D.C. That day he led a peace march of 250,000 people. They wanted to ensure the rights of the Constitution to all people in the United States.

He became famous and was loved and respected by many people all around the world. He received the Nobel Peace Prize in 1964. Martin Luther King died at the age of 39 years. He was killed by an **assassin**, James Earl Ray. It was a very sad day for the American people and the world.

I.   Match words with similar meanings

1. **memorial** _____   **a.** religious song
2. **clergyman** _____   **b.** killer
3. **segregate** _____   **c.** unfairness
4. **rights** _____   **d.** bringing groups of people
5. **racial** _____   together, combining
6. **injustice** _____   **e.** remembrance; something
7. **integration** _____   done to remember or honor
8. **assassin** _____   a person
9. **spiritual** _____   **f.** being unfair to a group of
10. **discrimination** _____   people because of their
                             color, religion, etc.
                          g. separate
                          h. ethnic
                          i. privileges
                          j. pastor; minister

II. Circle the word that will best complete each sentence.

1. Many people attend church (justice, memorial) services in honor of Martin Luther King.
2. Martin Luther King worked to end (segregation, ethnic) of black people; he believed that all men are equal.
3. He wanted people of all races to be (injustice, integrated).
4. Martin Luther King worked to end (discrimination, rights) against black people.

13

5. A person who kills is called an (assassination, assassin).

6. The (memorial, spiritual) "We Shall Overcome" is recognized as the Civil Rights Anthem.

7. The church memorial service in honor of Martin Luther King was conducted by a (spiritual, clergyman).

8. All people should believe that (racial, spiritual) differences are not important, but that all human beings have the same (segregation, rights).

9. People who fight for equality know that it is a(n) (segregation, injustice) to judge people by the color of their skin.

III. Select words to complete the sentences below.

1. Marian Anderson sang _____ and other songs in her concert.

2. It is an _____ to be punished for a crime you did not commit.

3. The _____ married four couples in one afternoon.

4. In the United States boys and girls are not _____ in public schools; they all are in the same class.

5. A large crowd attended the outdoor _____ service to remember and honor the heroes.

6. Men and women must have the same _____ since the Constitution guarantees equality for all.

7. Many different _____ groups can be found in New York City since people from all over the world come to live in the United States.

8. It is against the law for employers to _____ against employees because of their nationality.

9. The police found the _____ and he was brought to trial.

10. Public schools cannot separate boys and girls in different classes; they all have to be _____ .

IV. Complete these sentences.

1. The artist designed a monument to honor and remember the famous hero.

   He created a _____ .

2. On Martin Luther King's birthday people sang "We Shall Overcome."

   They sang a _____ .

3. "All men are created equal."

   This is a statement of _____ equality.

4. All youngsters from the age of 5 to 21 can go to public school.

   It is their _____ .

5. In the United States, students cannot be separated because of their race or religion.

   _____ is illegal.

V. Circle the word that does not belong.

1. clergyman   actor   minister   pastor
2. inequality   democracy   injustice   discrimination
3. separation   integration   combination   togetherness
4. killer   criminal   fireman   assassin
5. discrimination   unfairness   justice   inequality

VI. Can you match these famous black Americans with their professions?

1. Jackie Robinson _____ **a.** poet
2. Jessie Owens _____ **b.** opera singer
3. Joe Louis _____ **c.** actor
4. Alex Haley _____ **d.** baseball player
5. Ralph Bunche _____ **e.** musician-composer
6. Mohammed Ali _____ **f.** actress
7. Langston Hughes _____ **g.** scientist
8. Marian Anderson _____ **h.** Olympic athlete
9. Paul Robeson _____ **i.** singer
10. Robert McNair _____ **j.** boxer
11. Michael Jackson _____ **k.** diplomat
12. Harry Belafonte _____ **l.** astronaut
13. Alice Walker _____ **m.** writer
14. George Washington **n.** football player
    Carver _____
15. Lena Horne _____
16. Duke Ellington _____
17. Louis Armstrong _____
18. Ethel Waters _____
19. Bill Cosby _____

Traditions and Customs

Valentine's day is celebrated on February 14th as a **festival** of **romance** and **affection**. People send greeting cards called "valentines" to their **sweethearts**, friends, and members of their families.

Many valentines have romantic poems; others are **humorous**. But almost all valentines ask "Be My Valentine." This may mean be my friend or be my love or be my **companion**. Valentines often show a cupid with an arrow. Cupid, also called Eros, was the ancient Roman god of love.

Valentine's day is not a legal holiday; schools and banks are open as usual. **Merchants** sell valentines and **decorations** for Valentine's Day parties and dances. All the decorations are bright red, and the most popular ones are heart shaped.

School children decorate their classrooms with bright red paper hearts and celebrate the day in their classroom. They also make valentine cards for their friends and parents.

Stores advertise heavily for this holiday since it is traditional for sweethearts, **spouses**, and members of the family to exchange gifts on Valentine's Day. Heart shaped boxes of candy, jewelry and flowers are some of the popular gifts given on this day.

Many newspapers carry advertisements or messages placed by people in love. Both men and women want to let their sweethearts know how much they love them. On Valentine's Day, many radio stations play romantic music all day long. One very famous song is called "My Funny Valentine."

Valentine's Day is a day to share loving **feelings** with friends and family. It has become traditional for many couples to become engaged on this day. Also, famous couples are remembered. Some of them are Romeo and Juliet, Caesar and Cleopatra, among others. This is a happy day because it is specially dedicated to celebrate love, affection and friendship.

Background

Valentine's Day comes on the feast of two different Christian saints named Valentine. But the way that Valentine's Day is celebrated has nothing to do with the lives of the saints.

This celebration comes from an ancient Roman festival called "Lupercalia" which took place every February 15th. This festival honored Juno, the Roman goddess of women and marriage, and Pan the god of nature. It was also believed that birds choose their mates on this date. Valentine's Day became very popular in the United States in the 1800's.

I. Match words with similar meanings

1. **romance** ____ **a.** boyfriend; girlfriend
2. **affection** ____ **b.** love
3. **humorous** ____ **c.** tenderness; warm feelings
4. **decorate** ____ **d.** make attractive
5. **merchant** ____ **e.** wife or husband
6. **spouse** ____ **f.** emotions
7. **feelings** ____ **g.** funny
8. **companion** ____ **h.** celebration
9. **festival** ____ **i.** storekeeper
10. **sweetheart** ____ **j.** friend

II. Cross out the phrases or words that don't belong.

1. humorous — a. serious
                b. funny
                c. light-hearted
                d. comic
2. affection — a. a hug
                b. a kiss
                c. holding hands
                d. anger

19

3. merchant —
   a. customer
   b. salesperson
   c. seller
   d. florist

4. feelings —
   a. love
   b. anger
   c. homework
   d. happiness

5. companion —
   a. a person
   b. a friend
   c. a car
   d. a roommate

6. festival —
   a. a party
   b. a celebration
   c. a funeral
   d. a parade

7. sweetheart —
   a. boyfriend
   b. enemy
   c. wife
   d. husband

8. spouse —
   a. husband
   b. mate
   c. parent
   d. wife

9. decorations —
   a. paper hearts
   b. flowers
   c. pictures
   d. dresses

10. romance —
   a. relationship
   b. affair
   c. love
   d. fight

III. Select the word that best completes the sentence.

1. On the classroom walls there are (celebrations, decorations, festivals).
2. Valentine's Day is a celebration of love and (romance, decorations, parents).
3. Valentines cards have messages of (affection, humorous, share).
4. It is traditional to send flowers to (celebrate, spouses, dedicate) on Valentine's Day.
5. On this day people share feelings of affection with friends, family and (flowers, affection, companions).
6. (Sweethearts, spouses, merchants) decorate their stores with red hearts and cupids on Valentine's day.
7. This is a day to celebrate (feelings, humorous, decorations) of friendship and love.
8. Some Valentine cards are funny; they have (loving, humorous, romance) messages.
9. Lupercalia was an ancient Roman (sharing, god, festival).
10. Many people call people they love (sweetheart, romance, spouse).

IV. Fill in the blanks with appropriate words. (change into the past tense as needed).

1. Romeo and Juliet loved each other very much; but their parents didn't know it.

   They had a secret _____ .

2. The young man got married.

   Now he was a _____ .

3. Mary likes John very much.

   She has good _____ toward him.

4. The grandmother asked her grandchild to go with her on the trip to Washington.

   She asked her to be her traveling _____ .

5. The high-school students decided to have a large party to celebrate the Spring.

   It was a beautiful _____ .

6. Martin told Helene: "I have warm feelings for you."

   He feels _____ for her.

7. Everybody laughed when they heard the story.

   It was very _____ .

8. The couple was very much in love.

   They called each other _____ .

9. The owners of the stores formed a group association.

   It is a group of _____ .

V. Select the correct word form to complete each sentence.

Noun	**Adjective**.
romance	romantic
festival	festive
humor	humorous
decoration	decorated
affection	affectionate

1. It is a (romance, romantic) _____ poem.
2. The Spring party was a (festival, festive) _____ occasion.
3. The TV comedy was full of (humor, humorous) _____ .
4. The Christmas tree was (decorated, decoration) _____ with colored lights.
5. He wrote a message of (affection, affectionate) _____ .

VI. Match the famous couples

1. Carmen	____	a.	Bathsheba
2. Adam	____	b.	Josephine
3. Lady Di	____	c.	Jane
4. Napoleon	____	d.	Eve
5. David	____	e.	Prince Charles
6. John Lennon	____	f.	Don Jose
7. Miss Piggy	____	g.	Yoko
8. Tarzan	____	h.	Kermit the Frog
9. Grace Kelly	____	i.	Prince Rainier
10. Rhett Butler	____	j.	Orpheus
11. Cho-Cho-San	____	k.	Scarlet O'Hara
12. Sophia Loren	____	l.	Captain Pinkerton
13. Eurydice	____	m.	Carlo Ponti

23

Traditions and Customs

In February, the United States honors two great American presidents: Abraham Lincoln, on February 12th, and George Washington, on February 22nd. These two days are combined into one legal holiday on the third Monday in February, called Presidents' Day.

Both presidents have been honored in different ways. George Washington is the only president to have a state named after him. The nation's capital, Washington, D.C., also has his name. There are cities, towns, streets, schools, bridges, and parks named after both President Lincoln and President Washington. Both have famous memorials in Washington, D.C. Their portraits also appear on postage stamps, bills, and coins. Washington's house in Mount Vernon and Lincoln's home in Springfield, Illinois, have been made into museums.

Cherry pie is a traditional food for Washington's Birthday because of a popular legend. It is said that as a boy Washington **chopped** down his father's cherry tree. When asked by his father, he **admitted** to his **wrongdoing** and said "I cannot tell a lie."

Background

George Washington, known as the "Father of His Country" was born February 22nd, 1732, in Westmoreland County, Virginia.

Washington helped shape the beginning of the United States in three important ways. First, he was the commander in chief of the Continental Army that won **independence** for 13 British colonies from Great Britain in the Revolutionary War. Secondly, in 1787, Washington served as president of the Constitutional Convention that wrote the United States Constitution. Lastly, George Washington was the first **elected** president of the U.S. He was the only president to be elected **unanimously**. He served a second term of office and **refused** a third term. He died on December 14th, 1799, at Mount Vernon at the age of 67.

Lincoln was born on February 12th, 1809, in a log cabin in Kentucky. He was elected the 16th President of the United States. It is said that, if he had not lived, the United States might be two countries today, instead of one. Lincoln was president during a difficult period of American history. Just before he started his presidency, seven southern states broke away from the United States and started their own country. They called it the

25

Confederate States of America and elected their own president, Jefferson Davis. The country was divided and involved in a civil war. President Lincoln was able to end the **conflict** and **unite** the country.

President Lincoln is praised and remembered for his belief in democracy, in the equality of all men and his fight for freedom for all. He believed slavery to be a cruel and evil practice. His famous speech "The Gettysburg Address" expresses his **ideals**. It has become a lasting symbol of democracy for the American people.

On January 1st, 1863, President Lincoln issued the Emancipation Proclamation which freed the slaves. Two years later, the 13th Amendment of the Constitution ended slavery in all parts of the United States.

President Lincoln was assassinated on April 9th, 1865. He was shot to death while watching a play in Ford's theater in Washington, D.C. The assassin was John Wilkes Booth, an actor, who thought he was helping the South.

I.   Match words with similar meanings

1. **chop**   _____ **a.** say no
2. **admit**   _____ **b.** freedom
3. **wrongdoing**   _____ **c.** tell the truth
4. **elect**   _____ **d.** bring together
5. **refuse**   _____ **e.** choose
6. **conflict**   _____ **f.** with complete agreement
7. **independence** _____ **g.** fault
8. **ideal**   _____ **h.** cut
9. **unanimously** _____ **i.** problem
10. **unite**   _____ **j.** perfect

II. Cross out the word that does not belong.

1. chop
   a. meat
   b. wood
   c. milk
   d. onions

2. admit
   a. a mistake
   b. an error
   c. a fault
   d. a television

3. refuse
   a. a wall
   b. to eat
   c. a gift
   d. to sing

4. elect
   a. a president
   b. a spouse
   c. a senator
   d. a judge

5. unite
   a. people
   b. countries
   c. a dress
   d. states

6. a wrongdoing
   a. to help a sick person.
   b. to steal
   c. to hurt someone
   d. to lie

III. Select the word that best completes the sentence.

1. George Washington (planted, chopped down) a cherry tree when he was young.

2. President Lincoln was able to (ideal, unite) a country divided by slavery.

3. Lincoln's (ideals, independence) of democracy and freedom are admired by all people.

4. Washington couldn't lie; he (admitted, refused) chopping down his father's tree.

5. President Washington was (refused, elected) for a third term as president.

6. The civil war was a tragic (conflict, ideal) during Lincoln's presidency.

7. According to a legend, Washington felt guilty about his (election, wrongdoing).

8. Washington fought to gain the (independence, conflict) of the United States from England.

9. Lincoln was (refused, elected) the 16th president of the United States.

10. Washington was the only president of the United States to be elected (independently, unanimously).

IV. Select words to complete the sentences below.

1. The recipe said to cut the meat in very small pieces.

    The meat had to be _____ .

2. The young couple finally came together.

    They were _____ .

3. The friends talked about their problem instead of fighting.

    They solved their _____ .

4. The boys wanted the girl to represent the class.

    She was _____ to the job.

5. The young man told his friends he finally had met the girl of his dreams.

    She was his _____ .

6. The young man decided to move out of his parents house.

    He wanted his _____ .

7. The mother told the children to eat the spinach, but they did not want it.

    They _____ to eat it.

8. The driver was afraid to say that the accident was his fault.

    He did not _____ he was wrong.

9. While playing in the street, the boys broke a window with their football and ran away.

    They were scared to admit their _____ .

10. Everybody agreed Evelyn should be the treasurer.

    They elected her _____ .

V. Ask a question about each statement. The first word in each question has been written for you.

1. George chopped down a cherry tree.
   What _____ ?

2. He admitted his wrongdoing because he couldn't lie.
   Why _____ ?

3. Lincoln was president during the conflict of the Civil War.
   When _____ ?

4. Washington became very famous during the fight for independence.
   When _____ ?

5. President Washington was elected unanimously.
   Who _____ ?

6. President Lincoln united the northern states and the confederacy.
   What _____ ?

7. In "The Gettysburg Address" President Lincoln expresses his ideals of democracy.
   Where _____ ?

8. George Washington was the first elected president of the United States.
   Who _____ ?

9. President Washington refused a third term.
   What _____ ?

10. George Washington's wrongdoing was to chop down his father's cherry tree.
    What _____ ?

Traditions and Customs

On March 17th, many people in the United States commemorate St. Patrick, the patron saint of Ireland. New York City, where there are many people of Irish **descent**, holds the famous St. Patrick's Day parade. Bands, marchers, **celebrities** (especially politicians), and **bystanders** come to **participate**. More than 150,000 people march in the parade. Almost a million people line the streets to watch. A green stripe is painted down the center of Fifth Avenue, and the lights on top of the Empire State Building are turned green, the color that represents the Irish people.

Millions of real shamrocks are flown from Ireland to the United States. They are used for decorations. Everything turns green on St. Patrick's Day. Green and gold **pennants** and green balloons are sold by the hundreds. Children and adults wear something green, and shops prepare green food: green bread, green pasta, green ice cream, green milkshakes. People eat corned beef and cabbage, and drink Irish coffee. Irish songs can be heard throughout the day on the radio.

Background

In Ireland, St. Patrick's Day is a religious holiday. St. Patrick's date of birth is **estimated** to be around the year 389. He died on March 17th, the day when his memory is honored.

When Patrick was 16 years old, Irish pirates landed near his home in England. They **captured** him and took him as a slave to Ireland. There he worked and learned the Irish language, traditions, and way of life. Patrick, who had been born and raised in a Christian home, was troubled because the Irish worshiped many gods and spirits. He wanted to **convert** the Irish people to Christianity.

He was able to escape to France and to study to be a priest. After 14 years of study, in the year 432, the Pope sent him back to Ireland as a bishop.

Patrick traveled all across Ireland and established churches and schools. According to his followers he performed many **miracles**. A well known **legend** says that he drove the snakes out of Ireland. He was greatly loved by the Irish people.

This holiday in the United States has come to represent the Irish culture and the great contributions of its people to the United States. Last names beginning with "O'" like O'Reilly, and with "Mac," like MacDonald, are of Irish origin. Many famous politicians including Presidents Kennedy and Reagan are of Irish descent.

I. Match words with similar meanings

1. **celebrity** _____ a. to take away by force
2. **bystanders** _____ b. story
3. **participate** _____ c. calculate, determine the
4. **pennant** _____   size or number or value of
5. **estimate** _____   something.
6. **capture** _____ d. wonder; something out of
7. **convert** _____   the ordinary
8. **miracle** _____ e. take part
9. **legend** _____ f. famous person
10. **descent** _____ g. people who stand and look at
    something
    h. flag
    i. origin
    j. to change a person from one
    religion or idea into another

II. Select the word that best completes the sentence.

1. Hundreds of (bystanders, celebrities) are standing along the avenue to watch the parade.
2. The students from the school band (convert, participate) in the St. Patrick's Day parade.
3. Saint Patrick wanted to (convert, estimate) the Irish people to Christianity.
4. It is said that St. Patrick performed many (miracles, legends) in his lifetime.
5. Political (miracles, celebrities) join the celebration.
6. Green balloons and (pennants, estimate) are used for decorations on St. Patrick's Day.
7. It is (captured, estimated) that St. Patrick was born in the year 389.

8. St. Patrick was (captured, converted) from his home by Irish pirates.
9. President Kennedy's family was of Irish (descent, legend); they came from Ireland.
10. Driving the snakes out of Ireland is a (legend, miracle).

III. Fill in the blanks.

Saint Patrick's Day is celebrated with a famous parade in New York City where there are many people of Irish _____. Many well known _____ participate in this event. The streets are full of _____ who come to _____ in the celebration. Everybody likes to wear green clothes that day. Green _____ hang from many windows.

It is not known exactly when Patrick was born. It is _____ that he was born in 389. Patrick was taken away from his home as a young boy. He was _____ by Irish pirates. When he grew up he wanted the Irish people to abandon their worship of idols and to _____ to Christianity. After he studied religion he traveled across Ireland. People say that he did extraordinary things; he performed _____; and one _____ says that there are no snakes in Ireland today because St. Patrick drove them out.

IV. Use the best word to complete the sentences below. (Change to the past, as needed).

1. Rock _____ get paid a lot of money for their concerts.
2. A story that may or may not be true is a _____.

3. Many people were found alive after the earthquake; everybody said that it was a _____.
4. There is a mathematical formula to _____ pounds to kilograms.
5. The insurance investigator _____ how much money was lost in the fire; he said it was about $12,000.00.
6. When celebrities participate in a parade, thousands of _____ come to see them pass by.
7. A teacher wants all students to _____ in the lesson so she calls everybody to the front of the room.
8. After a long investigation the police _____ the criminal.
9. The school _____ was gold, blue and red.
10. He says he is _____ from George Washington.

V. Complete the columns with nouns, adjectives, or verbs.

	Noun	Adjective.	Verb
example:	*love*	*loved*	to **love**
1.	the **celebrity**	_____	to _____
2.	the _____	_____	to **participate**
3.	the _____	**estimated**	to _____
4.	the **conversion**	_____	to _____
5.	the **capture**	_____	to _____

VI. Cross out the word that doesn't belong.

1. bystanders   people   cars   crowds
2. facts   mysteries   legends   miracles
3. a sign   a pennant   a flag   an idea
4. to convert   to alter   to change   to observe

Traditions and Customs

People in the United States honor their parents with two special days: Mother's Day, on the second Sunday in May, and Father's Day, on the third Sunday in June. These days are set aside to show love and **respect** for parents. They **raise** their children and educate them to be responsible citizens. They give love and care. These two days offer an opportunity to think about the changing **roles** of mothers and fathers. More mothers now work outside the home. More fathers must help with child-care.

These two special days are celebrated in many different ways. On Mother's Day people wear carnations.

A red one **symbolizes** a living mother. A white one shows that the mother is dead. Many people **attend** religious services to honor parents. It is also a day when people whose parents are dead visit the cemetery. On these days families get together at home, as well as in restaurants. They often have outdoor barbecues for Father's Day. These are days of fun and good feelings and **memories**.

Another tradition is to give cards and gifts. Children make them in school. Many people make their own presents. These are **valued** more than the ones bought in stores. It is not the value of the gift that is important, but it is "the **thought** that counts." Greeting card stores, florists, candy makers, bakeries, telephone companies, and other stores do a lot of business during these holidays.

Background

Mother's Day was **proclaimed** a day for national observance by President Woodrow Wilson in 1915. Ann Jarvis from Grafton, West Virginia, had started the idea to have a day to honor mothers. She was the one who chose the second Sunday in May and also began the custom of wearing a carnation.

In 1909, Mrs. Dodd from Spokane, Washington, thought of the idea of a day to honor fathers. She wanted to honor her own father, William Smart. After her mother died, he had the responsibility of raising a family of five sons and a daughter. In 1910, the first Father's Day was observed in Spokane. Senator Margaret Chase Smith helped to **establish** Father's Day as a national commemorative day, in 1972.

I. Match words with similar meanings

1. **respect** _____   a. represent
2. **raise** _____   b. remembrances
3. **proclaim** _____   c. set; make permanent
4. **role** _____   d. bring up
5. **symbolize** _____   e. participate
6. **attend** _____   f. consideration, honor
7. **memories** _____   g. ideas
8. **thoughts** _____   h. cost; importance
9. **value** _____   i. declare
10. **establish** _____   j. a function a person has; responsibility

II. Select the word that best completes each sentence.

1. It is the responsibility of the parents to (symbolize, raise, smile at) their children.
2. Children must show (respect, memories, symbols) for their parents.
3. The traditional (raise, love, role) of mothers and fathers is changing.
4. Ann Jarvis wanted to (establish, work, respect) one day to honor mothers.
5. Most parents are not interested in the (respect, honor, value) of a gift from their children.
6. Mother's Day and Father's Day cards express loving (customs, thoughts, honors).
7. Most people who think about the past have happy (respect, memories, honor) of their parents.
8. Many families (attend, respect, establish) church services on Mother's Day.

9. President Wilson (honored, symbolized, proclaimed) a day to honor mothers.
10. A red carnation worn on Mother's Day (symbolizes, establishes, values) a living mother.

III. Complete the sentences below.

Mothers and fathers are very important people in any society. They _____ their children from babies to adults with love and care. They show their children the _____ they must play to be good citizens. They teach children to have consideration and _____ for others. Parents also make sure that children _____ school.

They work very hard to _____ a family. They try to set a good example, to _____ what is good for their children. In return parents do not ask for much. They do not care about the _____ of gifts from their children, but they are happy with the _____ behind the gifts. Most people have happy _____ of their parents. It is a good idea that two days were _____ to honor fathers and mothers.

IV. Complete sentences.

1. The actor played in different dramas from Shakespeare.
   He played many _____.
2. In the United States students go to school from September to June.
   They _____ school ten months a year.
3. The couple was happy looking at the pictures from their wedding.
   It brought them happy _____.

4. People smile when they want to show happiness.

   A smile _____ happiness.

5. The boy took care of the kittens since they were born.

   He _____ them.

6. The two women agreed on their vacation plans.

   They had the same _____ about it.

7. The Congress of the United States declared January 15th to honor Martin Luther King.

   They _____ it a national holiday.

8. The bank opened a new office in New York City.

   They _____ another office.

9. The child shows reverence and consideration to the grandmother.

   She _____ her.

10. The famous painting was sold for a large sum of money.

    The painting was very _____able.

V. Circle the word that does not belong.

1. to raise   to grow   to bring up   to destroy
2. to establish   to set   to break up   to settle down
3. to value   to respect   to honor   to dislike
4. to be absent   to participate   to attend   to be present
5. to symbolize   to mean   to be unrelated   to represent
6. books   remembrances   memories   thoughts
7. to tell   to declare   to be silent   to proclaim
8. thought   idea   action   concept
9. to value   to ignore   to appreciate   to like
10. group   function   role   job

40

Traditions and Customs

Memorial Day is a **patriotic** holiday in the United States. It is also called Decoration Day. It is a legal holiday in most states. Northern states celebrate it on May 30th. Southern states celebrate it on different dates, April 26th, May 10th, or June 3rd.

Memorial Day is a sad holiday. The country remembers men and women in the Armed Forces who died or were disabled in war or in the **service** of their country.

People place flowers, **artificial** poppies and flags on the graves of servicemen and servicewomen. There are ceremonies at Gettysburg National Military Park and at the Tomb of the Unknown Soldier in the National Cemetery in Arlington, Virginia. Tiny ships filled with flowers are placed on the Delaware River. Wreaths are set afloat at Pearl Harbor, near the **wreck** of the battleship "Arizona."

Many organizations take part in parades and special programs. Some of these groups are Veterans organizations, Boy Scouts, Girl Scouts, and fraternal groups. The programs often include a reading of Abraham Lincoln's "Gettysburg Address."

Background

Memorial Day began during the American Civil War to honor the soldiers who died during the war. Some southern women chose May 30th to decorate the graves of the soldiers with flowers. It is also believed that Cassandra Oliver Moncure, a woman of French **origin** from Virginia, chose this date because it is the "Day of the Ashes" in France. (This French Memorial Day marks the return of General Napoleon Bonaparte's remains to France from St. Helena). In 1868, General John A. Logan designated the day to honor the soldiers who died in the war by decorating their graves.

Since the end of World War I, Memorial Day has also been known as Poppy Day. The poppy has become the symbol of the **tragedy** of World War I and of the **renewal** of life because many of the battlefields of France bloomed with poppies. Little red paper poppies are sold to the public for the **benefit** of **disabled** and **needy** veterans. The money collected is used for medical and educational services. A tag on each poppy says: "Honor the dead by helping the living."

42

I. Select a definition that corresponds to these words.

1. **patriotic** ____ a. very poor
2. **disabled** ____ b. assistance
3. **service** ____ c. loving one's country
4. **artificial** ____ d. unable to function normally;
5. **wreck** ____   handicapped
6. **origin** ____ e. made by man
7. **needy** ____ f. very sad event, a disaster
8. **tragedy** ____ g. something that is destroyed
9. **renewal** ____ h. a new beginning
10. **benefit** ____ i. work done for others
                      j. background; place where a
                         person or thing comes from

II. Match these words to words that best show the opposite meaning.

1. **patriotic** ____ a. whole; not destroyed
2. **renewal** ____ b. rich
3. **needy** ____ c. ending
4. **tragedy** ____ d. unpatriotic
5. **artificial** ____ e. not handicapped
6. **disabled** ____ f. comedy
7. **wreck** ____ g. natural

43

III. Select a word that best completes the sentence.

1. People who cannot walk and need a wheelchair are (soldiers, disabled).
2. Memorial Day honors men and women who died in the (origin, service) of their country.
3. Poppies made out of paper are called (natural, artificial) flowers.
4. There are cermonies held at the (origin, wreck) of the ship Arizona.
5. Cassandra Oliver Moncure came from a French family; she is of French (tragedy, origin).
6. Wars are a terrible (tragedy, benefit) because lives and property are lost.
7. During Memorial Day money is collected for (patriotic, needy) veterans.
8. During Memorial Day radios play many (needy, patriotic) songs.
9. The poppy has become a symbol of tragedy and (benefit, renewal) because they bloomed after the destruction on the battlefields.
10. Many people give money for the (benefit, tragedy) of disabled veterans.

IV. Complete each sentence.

1. The veteran had a very sad life; it was a _____.
2. The school has been fixed with special elevators and doors for the wheelchairs of _____ students.
3. The truck came to pick up the broken parts of the _____ed car.

4. The Olympic Games are of Greek _____.
5. Some people who are allergic to fresh flowers buy _____ plastic plants.
6. Many old areas in New York are going through a _____ to make them more beautiful.
7. Many organizations work hard to get money for _____ children around the world
8. Many people give time and money to work for the _____ of sick children.
9. The National Anthem is a _____ song.
10. Both husband and wife worked in the _____ of the same company.

V. Write questions about the sentences below. The first word has been written for you.

1. Memorial Day is a patriotic holiday.
   a. What _____?
   b. What kind of _____?

2. Memorial Day originated during the Civil War to honor the war dead.
   a. What _____?
   b. When _____?
   c. Why _____?

3. The old man placed artificial flowers on his son's grave.
   a. What kind _____?
   b. Where _____?
   c. On whose _____?

4. They collected the money for the benefit of the needy.
   a. What _____?
   b. Why _____?
   c. For whom _____?

Traditions and Customs

On July 4th, the United States celebrates Independence Day. It is a legal holiday. It is called Independence Day because on July 4th, 1776, the Continental Congress **declared** that the United States of America would become free and **independent** from England.

Many activities are organized to celebrate this holiday. All across America firecrackers are exploded and fireworks are displayed. They symbolize the gunpowder of the American revolution. Bands play patriotic marches in parades. Politicians make speeches about freedom and American ideals.

There are patriotic readings and music at various parks. People **organize** street fairs. Planes from the Air Force perform acrobatics in the air. Picnics, clambakes and barbecues are very popular activities on this day. Many families and friends celebrate the day at beaches, pools and baseball games. The lights of the Empire State building in New York City display the colors of the American flag: red, white and blue. In Monticello, Thomas Jefferson's home in Charlottesville, Virginia, Independence Day is observed with a **naturalization** ceremony. Newly naturalized citizens are **sworn in** and honored. A similar ceremony was held at the **rededication** of the Statue of Liberty in 1986. At that celebration, millions of people watched a parade of tall sailing ships and a huge fireworks display over New York harbor.

Background

In 1773, there were 13 English colonies in America, where more than 2 million people lived. England owned and governed the colonies. England tried to collect more money from the colonies by passing tax laws. These taxes made the Americans very angry. They said it was not fair for England to make them pay taxes that they did not vote on. The Americans said, "No taxation without **representation**."

One of the most hated taxes was a tax on tea. When three English ships loaded with tea docked in Boston Harbor, some Americans dressed as Indians threw all the tea into the water. This became known as the "Boston Tea Party."

England sent soldiers to America to **force** the colonists to **obey** English laws. English soldiers killed Americans in what is called the Boston Massacre.

It was finally decided at the Continental Congress that Americans should declare their independence from England. The Congress chose Benjamin Franklin, John Adams, Robert Livingston, and Roger Sherman to work on this idea. Thomas Jefferson was chosen to write the Declaration of Independence. It was signed on July 4th, 1776. Copies of the Declaration of Independence were read throughout the colonies. In Philadelphia, the Liberty Bell was rung to call the people to hear the reading.

After 7 years of war with England, the American colonies finally won and were **recognized** as a united, independent nation.

I.   Match words and phrases with similar meanings.

1. **to declare** _____
2. **independent** _____
3. **sworn** _____
4. **representation** _____
5. **to obey** _____
6. **to organize** _____
7. **naturalization** _____
8. **to force** _____
9. **rededication** _____
10. **to recognize** _____

a. standing in for someone else
b. to do what others want you to do
c. to arrange; to establish
d. to tell openly, formally
e. to govern oneself; free
f. promised; pledged
g. to accept; acknowledge
h. becoming a citizen
i. to make something happen using strength
j. to reopen a public building with ceremony.

II. Circle the word that best completes each sentence.

1. The Continental Congress (declared, obeyed, represented) the independence of the American Colonies on July 4th, 1776.

2. England wanted the American colonies to (represent, obey, rededicate) its laws.

3. People (force, organize, swear) many activities to celebrate Independence Day.

4. The American colonies wanted to be (naturalized, represented, independent) from England.

5. Many aliens become citizens and are (sworn in, organized, rededicated) in Monticello on Independence Day.

6. The American colonies did not want taxes without (declaration, representation, organization).

7. Every year there is a (declaration, organization, naturalization) ceremony in Monticello.

8. After the Declaration of Independence, the United States wanted to be (recognized, obeyed, naturalized) as an independent nation.

9. A (naturalization, organization, rededication) ceremony of the Statue of Liberty was organized in 1986.

10. England sent troops to (organize, obey, force) the American colonies to obey its laws.

III. Complete sentences below.

1. The candidate told the reporters that she was going to run for president.

   She _____ her intentions.

2. The family went to the ceremony where they became citizens of the United States.

   They went to the _____ ceremony.

3. The City Hall building was reopened and many activities were organized to celebrate it.

   There was a _____ ceremony.

4. The child did not want to come home for lunch. Finally the mother made him come.

   She had to _____ him to come to lunch.

5. When the group of tourists saw the building they said "It is the Empire State Building."

   They _____ it.

6. The people of the island want to have their own government.

   They want to be _____.

7. The governor could not go to the rededication ceremony so he sent his assistant in his place.

   The assistant _____ed the governor.

8. The new citizens promised to respect the Constitution of the United States.

   They were _____ as citizens.

9. "Antonio, you have to do what your mother says," said the father.

   Father wants Antonio to _____ him.

10. Anna prepared a list of guests, invited the people, and bought the decorations for the party.

    She _____ it.

50

IV. Cross out the word that doesn't belong.

1. declare   tell   announce   question
2. delegate   nobody   senator   representative
3. alien   citizen   American   naturalized
4. identify   recognize   forget   know
5. power   weakness   force   strength
6. opening   closing   beginning   rededication
7. do as told   obey   follow   disobey
8. organize   put in order   destroy   arrange
9. separate   independent   free   dependent
10. sworn   promised   disagreed   agreed

V. Complete each sentence below.

1. Every state has _____ in Congress.
2. To drive safely you must _____ traffic rules.
3. It is easy to find what you want here. It is well
   _____.
4. The famous actor wore dark glasses and a wig
   because he did not want to be _____.
5. The police took the criminal by _____.
6. The museum was closed for five months while they
   were fixing it. Now they are organizing a _____
   celebration.
7. The groom _____ his love for the bride in front
   of everybody.
8. Now that Norma is _____, she can make her
   own decisions.
9. Mrs. Martinez is studying to become a citizen. She
   hopes to have her _____ papers soon.
10. The spy was _____ to secrecy.

51

Traditions and Customs

Labor Day is a legal holiday. It is celebrated each year on the first Monday in September. It was planned as a day to honor workers in America and to give them a long weekend holiday from work.

Labor Day is traditionally celebrated with parades, speeches, and recognition of the labor **unions**. Labor Day sales are a popular event held on this holiday. Barbecues and picnics are popular on Labor Day. They mark the end of the summer season. Schools usually open after this holiday.

The unions want the public to know that the workers of America do an excellent job. Newspaper, magazine.

radio, and television advertisements bring the **message** to the people: "Look for the Union Label," which means the product was made by workers who belong to a union.

Background

Labor Day was started in 1882 by a union called the Knights of Labor. The first celebration was a long parade followed by a picnic in New York City. In 1894 Congress made it a legal holiday.

In America workers were not always treated well. In the early days of the 1800's hundreds of thousands of immigrants from Europe came to the United States. They worked for very little pay. The owners of businesses and factories were able to get a lot of work for little money. They expected their employees to work 10 to 16 hours a day. Women and children worked cheaper than men, and owners **hired** them for this reason.

In the 1880's, a fight for the workers was led by men who were workers themselves. They organized the workers in labor unions. The American Federation of Labor (AFL) was organized in 1886. Later the Congress of Industrial Organizations (CIO) was founded. **Wages**, hours of labor, and working conditions have improved since that time. Labor unions have **persuaded** the government and the states to pass laws that limit how many hours a week men and women can be **required** to work and tell what the **minimun** wage should be. They have determined that child labor, as well as discrimination based on sex,

53

religion, color, and national origin is now illegal. **Strikes** occur when people feel that there is wrongdoing. Everybody hopes for a fair and quick end of a strike.

American employers and workers of today face the problems of automation and **competition** of goods made in foreign countries where wages and costs are lower. Labor unions are helping to find **solutions** to protect American workers.

I.   Match words with similar meanings.

1. **strike**   _____ **a.** salary
2. **to hire**   _____ **b.** to need; to demand
3. **wages**   _____ **c.** convince
4. **persuade**   _____ **d.** smallest possible
5. **to require**   _____ **e.** answer to a problem
6. **minimum**   _____ **f.** to give a job
7. **union**   _____ **g.** information
8. **competition**   _____ **h.** stopping of work
9. **solution**   _____ **i.** rivalry; contest
10. **message**   _____ **j.** organization of workers

II. Select the word that best completes each sentence.

1. "Look for the Union Label" is a (solution, message) from the unions.
2. Employers cannot (hire, improve) children to work.
3. Cars from Europe create (strikes, competition) for American workers.
4. Unions fought to have fair (wages, minimum) for all workers.
5. Labor unions work to find (messages, solutions) to the problems of American workers.

54

6. It is not legal to pay workers less than the (organized, minimum) wage.

7. The unions (persuaded, hired) the government to create laws to protect the workers.

8. Workers sometimes (strike, persuade) when they are unhappy about their salary.

9. (Improvements, Unions) are organizations made up of workers.

III. Complete these sentences.

1. The girl told her mother what her father had said.
She gave the mother the _____.

2. The mechanic fixed the problem with the car.
He found the _____.

3. The nurses are not working today because they are protesting against the long hours of work.
They are on _____.

4. The company needed some new workers.
They _____ two men and three women.

5. The worker went to the office on Friday to get paid.
He went to get his _____.

6. The teenager explained to his father why he needed the car, and finally convinced his father.
The teenager _____ his father.

7. Men have to wear a jacket and tie to go into that restaurant.
Ties and jackets are _____.

8. In some banks, people need at least $300 to open a savings account.
The bank asks for a _____ amount of money.

9. The new worker became a member of the worker's organization.
He joined the _____.

10. Both stores sell the same merchandise and they fight for the same customers.
They are in _____.

55

IV. Circle the word that does not belong.

1. to hire   to rent   to contract   to dismiss
2. to work   to strike   to protest   to demonstrate
3. salary   wages   work   fee
4. letter   message   communication   to know
5. to convince   to ignore   to influence   to persuade
6. competition   fight   agreement   conflict
7. solution   problem   agreement   answer
8. minimum   least   smallest   maximum
9. to demand   to need   to know   to require
10. union   organization   individual   group

V. Select the word that best completes each sentence.

hiring persuading requiring striking competing

1. Some high school students are trying to get a job at the supermarket.
   The supermarket is _____ new cashiers.
2. There are now smoking and non-smoking sections in restaurants.
   The law is now _____ places for smokers and non-smokers
3. The teachers stopped working because they want more money.
   They are _____ outside the school.
4. "Look for the Union Label" is a message played on TV and radio.
   The union is _____ people to buy products made by union workers in America.
5. American companies are now making smaller cars.
   They are _____ with foreign cars.

56

Traditions and Customs

Columbus Day is celebrated on October 12th. It commemorates the discovery of America by Christopher Columbus on October 12, 1492.

It is a legal holiday. Schools, banks, post offices and government offices are closed. Many schools hold programs and special events. Cities and organizations sponsor ceremonies, parades, fairs, food festivals, and banquets.

Traditionally this is a day to celebrate the **contributions** to the culture of the United States made by

Italian immigrants. Pizza and pasta, opera, and Italian fashion are part of the daily life of Americans.

It is also a day to recognize the strong **ties** of friendship between the two countries: Italy and the United States. Italian-American politicians and entertainers participate in many public events and TV programs.

Many sales are held throughout the USA on Columbus Day since all the stores are open.

Background

Christopher Columbus was born in the seaport of Genoa, Italy. Columbus heard sailors speak of Marco Polo who had visited the Far East 200 years earlier. He wrote about his long voyage by land and the wonders he had seen.

Columbus wanted to find a shorter **route** to Japan, China, India and the East Indies. Europeans were very interested in the gold, gems and spices that came from the East. They used camels, horses, and elephants to travel on land, across mountains and deserts to get to these countries. These trips were long, dangerous, and expensive.

At that time, many people thought that the world was flat. They said that if a ship would sail to the edge of the world, it would fall off and be lost. Columbus did not believe this; he was always **convinced** that the world was round.

King Ferdinand and Queen Isabella of Spain agreed to **finance** Columbus' **expeditions**. On the third of August, 1492, Columbus set sail with three ships, the Santa Maria, the Pinta, and the Niña. These ships were made of wood and had very few **comforts**. The ships had compasses, but they were **crude**. Columbus **navigated** by studying the stars and the moon.

It was a dangerous voyage. Nobody had ever sailed so long without seeing land. Finally, on October 12th, they saw an island. Columbus believed he had discovered an island off the East Indies. He was wrong. He really had discovered a new world: America. He called this island San Salvador and the natives there Indians, because he was sure San Salvador was in the Indies.

As a seaman, he was one of the greatest in history. He not only discovered a new world, but his success **encouraged** other explorers. Later, because of Columbus, other sailors did find a new way to get to India.

I.   Match words or phrases with similar meanings.

1. **contribution** _____ **a.** a way; a road
2. **tie** _____ **b.** to provide money
3. **crude** _____ **c.** to persuade someone to do or think something
4. **to encourage** _____
5. **route** _____ **d.** something given to others
6. **navigate** _____ **e.** to give help, courage, confidence
7. **to finance** _____
8. **to convince** _____ **f.** something that holds people together
9. **expedition** _____
10. **comfort** _____ **g.** no pain; no worry

h. not refined; not carefully made;

i. to direct a ship or a plane.

j. a trip of exploration.

II. Circle the word that best completes each sentence.

1. King Ferdinand and Queen Isabella (traveled, financed, convinced) Columbus' expedition.
2. Columbus was (comforted, navigated, convinced) that the world was round.
3. On Columbus Day we also celebrate the (contributions, expeditions, routes) of the Italian culture and people.
4. There are (routes, comforts, ties) of friendship between Italy and the United States.
5. The instruments used in Columbus' expeditions were (comfortable, crude, financial).
6. The success of Columbus' travels (encouraged, comforted, routed) other explorers.
7. Columbus wanted to find a sea (navigation, tie, route) to the Indies.
8. The ships used for Columbus expeditions had no (routes, comforts, finances).
9. Columbus (convinced, encouraged, navigated) his ships by studying the stars.
10. The King and Queen of Spain financed Columbus' (expedition, route, contribution).

III. Complete the paragraph.

Columbus was an explorer. He wanted to find a sea-route to the Indies. He needed money so he talked to the King and Queen of Spain and _____ them to _____ his voyage. With the money, he got ships, equipment, and sailors for the _____. The ships did not have many _____. The compasses were not sophisticated. With the _____ compasses and the help of stars, Columbus _____ the ships. He did not get to the East Indies but he discovered a new world. His expeditions _____ other explorers to organize other expeditions.

60

IV. Cross out the word that doesn't belong.

1. Things to contribute to a party:
   a. money
   b. paper plates
   c. food
   d. sadness

2. Ties between friends:
   a. affection
   b. fights
   c. secrets
   d. understanding

3. Who can encourage?
   a. a parent
   b. a friend
   c. a teacher
   d. a competitor

4. You can organize an expedition to:
   a. your house
   b. a new island
   c. the moon
   d. the Arctic

5. Somebody who can finance a new business:
   a. a banker
   b. a rich person
   c. a businessman
   d. an explorer

6. You can convince:
   a. an argument
   b. your friend
   c. your husband or wife
   d. a teacher

7. Things related to comfort.
   a. noise
   b. beautiful music
   c. soft bed
   d. a quiet home

8. You can navigate:
   a. a ship
   b. a plane
   c. a bicycle
   d. a spacecraft

9. To be crude is to be:
   a. very simple
   b. not well made
   c. refined and sophisticated
   d. unrefined

10. You need to know the route:
    a. to stay home
    b. to go on a trip
    c. to drive from Texas to Maine
    d. to sail from N.Y. to the Bahamas

V. Complete each sentence.

1. The music of Elvis Presley is part of American culture.

    Elvis made a _____ to American culture.

2. The father is giving confidence to his daughter by helping her learn to ride a bicycle.

    He is _____ her.

3. Albert is learning how to direct a plane.

    He is learning how to _____.

4. The young woman wants someone to give her money to start her business.

    She wants someone to _____ her business.

5. They are preparing the tools, maps, food, and instruments for the exploration trip.

    They are going on an _____.

6. Nancy didn't want to go out, but Rosa talked to her so much that they finally went to the park.

    Rosa _____ Nancy.

7. The hotel was in a quiet place; the rooms were large, and they had a pool and a restaurant.

    The hotel had many _____.

8. The couple got a map and found the way to go from New York to Washington.

    They found the _____.

9. Roger and Martin were friends for many years. They shared many things in their life.

    There were strong _____ between them.

10. The room only had a table and one chair and no other comforts.

    It was very _____.

Traditions and Customs

Halloween is a festival celebrated on October 31st. The name of the holiday means "hallowed" or "**holy** evening" because it happens the day before All Saints Day.

It is said that Halloween is the children's New Year's Eve. They dress up with special **costumes**, they eat too much, and stay up too late celebrating.

Children go around the neighborhood wearing make-up, and dressed in masks and colorful costumes. The most common costumes are witches, **ghosts**, skeletons, and popular TV, movie, and storybook **characters**. Some costumes are homemade; others are bought in stores. The children go door to door saying "**trick** or **treat**." People give them candy, cookies, fruit, or money. Sometimes money is **collected** to help UNICEF (United Nations International Children's Emergency Fund).

63

Homes, stores, and classrooms are decorated in the traditional Halloween colors, orange and black. Usual decorations are witches, black cats, ghosts, skeletons, and jack-o-lanterns. Jack-o-lanterns are pumpkins that are **carved** to look like faces. They are placed on doorway entrances and in windows. Horror movies and ghost stories are shown on TV on this day.

Adults and older children also celebrate Halloween with parades, festivals, and costume parties. Some people create their costumes; other people rent them. Contests are held where the best costume receives a prize. One of the party events popular with children is dunking for apples. Apples are put in tubs filled with water. People try to get the apples using only their mouths; hands cannot be used.

Background

Halloween comes the day before "All Saints Day." Many superstitions are connected with this day. The Druids, a group of priests from Gaul and Britain, believed that ghosts, spirits, and witches came out to harm people on Halloween. It is because of this legend that people place jack-o-lanterns, and **scary** decorations in front of their homes to scare **evil** spirits away. The Druids also thought that cats were sacred. They believed that they were once humans who were changed into animals because they did evil things. That is why black cats are part of Halloween. It is also believed that the pumpkin symbolizes the human skull.

I. Match words and phrases with similar meanings.

1. **trick** _____ a. a person in a story, novel, play
2. **to carve** _____ b. something harmful, bad
3. **character** _____ c. a gift; something nice
4. **collect** _____ d. a practical joke
5. **evil** _____ e. frightening
6. **holy** _____ f. to form something by cutting
7. **ghost** _____ g. sacred
8. **costumes** _____ h. to get; obtain
9. **scary** _____ i. special dress
10. **treat** _____ j. dead person's spirit

II. Circle the word that best completes the sentence.

1. On Halloween pumpkins are (carved, costumed, scary) to look like a face.
2. Some children dress like television (groups, characters, sets).
3. Children dress up to look like (tricks, saints, ghosts).
4. On Halloween you can see (collect, trick, scary) movies on TV.
5. Halloween means (evil, holy, scary) evening.
6. Children wear colorful (ghosts, characters, costumes) on Halloween.
7. Some children may play (tricks, treats, carve) on Halloween.

8. Some children (carve, trick, collect) money for UNICEF on Halloween.

9. People put scary decorations in front of their doors to scare (sacred, holy, evil) spirits away.

10. People give children (treats, tricks, costumes) when they come to the door.

III. Complete each sentence.

1. The girl bought a special dress for the party.
   She bought a _____.

2. The child dressed up like a dead person.
   She wore a _____ costume.

3. When the birthday person opened the empty box, his friends laughed.
   It was a _____.

4. Martin liked to take a piece of wood and make a horse, cutting away with his knife.
   He liked to _____.

5. The book told a story about three people.
   The story had three _____.

6. One of the characters in the story was a bad, mean woman.
   She was _____.

7. The Bible is a religious book.
   It is a _____ book.

8. John has dozens of costumes.
   He has a fine _____ion of costumes.

9. The storm made everybody afraid.
   It was _____.

10. The father bought his son a large ice cream.
    That was a real _____ for the child.

IV. Complete the puzzle with words which mean the same as these words.

1. group
2. dress
3. person in a story
4. no danger
5. frightening
6. joke
7. bad

V. What are they doing? Complete each sentence with the words below.

carving   trick or treating   scaring   collecting

1. The teacher is cutting out a face on the pumpkin.
   She is _____ the pumpkin.
2. The children are putting the candy and money in a shopping bag.
   They are _____ the candy and money.
3. Children are going door to door on Halloween.
   They are _____.
4. Some people hang black cats and ghosts on their doors.
   They are _____ away evil spirits.

Voting Requirements and Procedures

The first Tuesday after the first Monday in November is **Election** Day. It is a legal holiday. Since 1845, by Act of Congress, this date has been set aside for elections.

On this day American citizens elect their public officials, president, congressmen, governors, mayors and judges. A president is elected every four years, congressmen every two years and senators every six years. In some election years, people can also **vote** on issues of public interest.

All states require that voters be citizens of the United States. They can be born in the country or naturalized. They have to be 18 years old by election day. They must have a voter **registration** card and live for a certain amount of time in the state, county and precinct where they vote.

Polls are places where people go to vote. Polls are held in public buildings. The hours and place are **advertised** on radio, TV, and newspapers. At the polling place, election supervisors check the voter's identification. The voter then enters the voting booth. Inside the booth there is often a voting machine. There he votes alone and in secret, in the **privacy** of the voting booth. The names of the **candidates** and their political party are listed on the machine. The voter chooses the candidate and then the machine counts the vote. Voting machines are helpful in getting fast **results** without mistakes. Candidates receiving the most votes are elected.

"Election Day" sales in stores are very popular on this day. The night of the election, people watch the election results on TV. They listen to the speeches made by the winners.

Background

The United States has two big political parties: the Democrats, symbolized by a donkey, and the Republicans, symbolized by an elephant. There are also several smaller parties. Each party has its own ideas about what is best for the country. The time before an election is when candidates **campaign**. They explain what they think and what should be done. Candidates try to get the voter to vote for them.

This is also the time when it is the **duty** of the voters to find out as much as they can about the candidates and their plans. This can be done by listening to radio and TV news and **debates**, and by reading newspapers.

I.   Match words or phrases of similar meanings.

1. **election** _____
2. **to vote** _____
3. **duty** _____
4. **registration** _____
5. **privacy** _____
6. **advertise** _____
7. **candidate** _____
8. **result** _____
9. **campaign** _____
10. **debate** _____

a. an organized plan of action
b. what happened at the end
c. the process of choosing leaders
d. to express what you want by choosing
e. a formal discussion or argument
f. obligation
g. enrollment; be put on an official list
h. not in public; secret
i. to tell people about something
j. a person who wants to be elected

II.   Circle the word that best completes the sentence.

1. The candidates for president usually discuss their ideas in a public (election, debate, result).
2. You have to wait for an (election, voter, campaign) to vote for a candidate.
3. After the election people watch the (voters, advertisements, results) of the election on TV.

70

4. Candidates state their ideas during their (campaign, election, privacy).

5. People who want to be elected are called (voters, candidates, advertisers).

6. People who want to (advertise, campaign, vote) during the elections have to be citizens.

7. Before the election it is the (duty, result, privacy) of the voters to find out about the candidates.

8. Newspapers, radio and television (debate, vote, advertise) the date and time of the elections.

9. When voters go to the polls they must bring their (election, voting, registration) cards.

10. Voting is done in (campaigns, debates, private); nobody can see what the voter does.

III. Complete each sentence with words from the vocabulary.

1. Election Day is in November. Newspapers, radio and television _____ the date and hours of the voting. On that day voters go with their cards to _____ for their favorite candidate. Voting is done inside a voting booth. Nobody can see who the person is voting for; voting is done in _____.

Before _____ Day, candidates work hard in their _____ trying to get the people to vote for them. Sometimes _____ have a debate on television before the election. It is important to hear the debate and to find out as much a possible about the candidates and their ideas; it is the _____ of the voters to know about the candidates. With the help of voting machines and computers the _____ of the election can be heard and seen on the same night of the election.

IV. Cross out the word that does not belong.

1. choose   elect   vote   not decide
2. poll   candidate   politician   campaigner
3. privacy   secrecy   alone   public
4. result   citizen   the end   consequence
5. plan   strategy   campaign   organization
6. duty   job   obligation   irresponsibility
7. debate   argument   discussion   advertisement
8. advertise   tell   keep secret   promote

V. Complete each sentence.

1. It is the _____ of parents to take care of their children.

2. You'll have to sign up for that on _____ day.

3. The young girl wanted _____ so she closed the door to her room.

4. The children were playing outside all day, and as a _____ they were very tired.

5. The city organized a _____ to clean up the streets and parks.

6. The decision was unanimous; everybody _____ for him.

7. We don't have any candidates so there won't be an _____.

8. One student from each class participated in the _____ before the election.

9. There are two _____ for class president.

10. Makers of toys _____ in children's magazines and television programs.

72

Traditions and Customs

Veterans Day is a legal holiday celebrated on November 11th. It is a day to **remember** and **honor** all those Americans who **served** in the armed forces and particularly those who fought during the Spanish-American War, World Wars I and II, the Korean War, and the Vietnam War. People also remember those soldiers **missing** in action. This day reminds people of the **courage** and patriotism of all men and women who serve their country.

Veterans Day is **observed** in special programs or in church services. Services are held at the tomb of the Unknown Soldier in Arlington National Cemetery. There are wreath-laying **ceremonies** at war monuments and cemeteries throughout the nation.

It is a day when many people visit famous memorials, such as the Vietnam Veterans Memorials in Washington and in New York and the United States Marine Corps War Memorial in Washington.

Veterans groups organize barbecues, picnics, and dances. Store sales are very popular on this holiday.

Background

President Woodrow Wilson proclaimed November 11th as Armistice Day so Americans would not forget the tragedies of war. Great Britain and France celebrate this day to commemorate the end of fighting of World War I on November 11th, 1918. On November 11th, 1921, the body of an American soldier killed in World War I was **buried** in the "Tomb of the Unknown Soldier" in Arlington National Cemetery in Washington, D.C. On the tomb are these words: "Here rests in honored glory an American soldier known but to God."

A law **enacted** in 1938 made the day a federal holiday. In 1954 Congress changed the name to Veterans Day to honor all United States veterans. It is also a day **dedicated** to world peace.

I. Match words or phrases of similar meanings.

1. **remember** _____
2. **to enact** _____
3. **courage** _____
4. **missing** _____
5. **to observe a holiday** _____
6. **bury** _____
7. **to be dedicated** _____
8. **to honor** _____
9. **to serve** _____
10. **ceremony** _____

a. no fear; valor; bravery
b. to celebrate
c. to place a dead person in a grave
d. to think of somebody or something; to be reminded
e. to make official or legal
f. a formal occasion or service
g. to work for
h. to have a single purpose
i. to give respect
j. lost, absent

II. Circle the word or phrase that does not belong.

1. remember   remind   forget   think about
2. lost   absent   missing   found
3. hide   bury   bring out   cover up
4. establish   approve   deny   enact
5. insult   honor   respect   love
6. valor   bravery   fear   courage
7. observe   forget   celebrate   commemorate
8. ceremony   service   rite   incident
9. work for   be dedicated   care   be uninterested
10. help   serve   work for   avoid

III. Circle the word that best completes the sentence.

1. On Veterans Day Americans (remember, bury, observe) veterans who served in the Armed forces.

2. Men and women can (exercise, serve, shop in) their country in different ways.

75

3. People who fight for their country have (service, work, courage); they are not afraid.

4. After the war, many soldiers could not be found; they are (buried, dedicated, missing).

5. Laying the wreath on the tomb was part of a very solemn (observation, honor, ceremony).

6. Veterans Day is (honored, named, observed) on November 11th in the United States.

7. The body of an American soldier is (named, buried, dedicated) in the Tomb of the Unknown Soldier in Arlington.

8. Many people all over the world are (named, celebrated, dedicated) to peace.

9. On Veterans Day the United States (honors, buries, misses) Americans who served and fought for their country.

10. Veterans Day was established as a federal holiday by a law (enacted, named, observed) in 1938.

IV. Complete the sentences.

1. On Veterans Day people also think about soldiers who did not come back or who could not be found.

   These are called soldiers _____ in action.

2. An American soldier was placed in the Tomb of the Unknown Soldier.

   He was _____ in the tomb.

3. In 1938, Congress decided by law to observe Veterans Day on November 11th.

   They _____ the law.

4. Veterans Day is a day to think about people who served their country.

   It is a day to _____ them.

5. On this day, people remember that men and women serving their country are brave.

   They have _____ .

76

6. Many people cried at the service.

   It was a sad and moving _____.

7. Veterans Day is celebrated with religious services, public ceremonies, and other events.

   It is _____ in many different ways.

8. Many organizations are working for peace in the world.

   They are _____ to world peace.

9. A soldier, a nurse, a teacher, a scientist can all work to help their country.

   They all _____ their country.

10. Most Americans give respect and thanks to those who serve the country.

    They _____ them.

V. Complete these sentences.

   1. Sometimes it is hard to _____ family birthdays. Many people write them in a book so they won't forget.

   2. Sonia could not find her keys; they were _____.

   3. Dogs like to _____ bones in the ground.

   4. Some famous singers and artists work very hard for needy people. They are _____ to helping others.

   5. People who climb mountains have no fear; they have a lot of _____.

   6. Before a law can be _____, Congress has to vote on it.

   7. To _____ your parents, you must show respect and love.

   8. Most people in the United States _____ the end of the old year and the start of the new with a party.

   9. The _____ was very short; only fifteen minutes.

   10. In the United States you have to be at least 18 years old to _____ in the Armed Forces.

Traditions and Customs

Thanksgiving Day comes on the 4th Thursday in November. It is a legal holiday celebrated throughout the United States. People of all **faiths** celebrate this day. They give thanks for the many good things in their lives.

78

This is a family holiday. Families come together from near and far. In some places special religious services are held in the morning. Then comes the traditional **feast**. Turkey with **stuffing** is the main dish. It is served with sweet potatoes, squash, cranberry sauce, and pumpkin pie. Apple cider is the drink of the day.

Football is the most popular game on this day. For many schools, the Thanksgiving Day game is the most important one of the year. Usually there are several football games to watch on TV.

Macy's department store holds its **annual** Thanksgiving Day Parade in New York City. Celebrities, floats, bands, and balloons shaped like famous storybook and cartoon characters appear in the parade. Santa Claus arrives at the end. His coming marks the beginning of the Christmas season.

Stores, classrooms, and homes are decorated with turkeys, pilgrims, Indians, **wreaths** of dried flowers, and vegetables. Horns of plenty are also very popular.

Charitable organizations serve dinners to needy people. They also send baskets of food to the **elderly** and sick.

Background

The first Thanksgiving Day was celebrated by the Pilgrims on 1621. They came from England for religious freedom. They sailed from Plymouth, England, on September 16, 1620. Their ship was called the Mayflower. They landed at Plymouth Rock, in Massachusetts, on December 26, 1620.

The first winter was a terrible time. There was much sickness and **starvation**. Native Indians taught the Pilgrims how to plant, to fish, to hunt and how to **survive** in America. The crops did well, and in the fall of 1621 the Pilgrims had a great **harvest**. They were very thankful and decided to celebrate with a feast. The Pilgrims invited their Indian friends to share this Thanksgiving feast.

Thanksgiving was proclaimed a national day of **observance** by Congress in 1941.

I.   Match words or phrases of similar meanings.

1. **annual**	_____	**a.** to stay alive
2. **elderly**	_____	**b.** a large meal, a banquet
3. **feast**	_____	**c.** religions
4. **harvest**	_____	**d.** a circular arrangement of
5. **observance**	_____	flowers or dried flowers
6. **faiths**	_____	**e.** hunger
7. **starvation**	_____	**f.** happening every year
8. **stuffing**	_____	**g.** putting food inside meat
9. **survive**	_____	or vegetables
10. **wreath**	_____	**h.** people of old age
		i. the collection of crops (fruits, vegetables).
		j. the celebration of a holiday

II. Circle the word that does not belong.

1. flowers   arrangement   wreath   food
2. hunger   starvation   need   abundance
3. annual   yearly   weekly   every 12 months
4. young   mature   old   elderly
5. harvest   collection   planting   gathering crops
6. celebration   observance   forgetting   ceremony
7. religions   games   faiths   beliefs
8. alive   survive   die   exist
9. banquet   feast   starvation   meal
10. stuffing   food   filling   reading

III. Circle the word that best completes each sentence.

1. On Thanksgiving some organizations prepare food for the needy and the (stores, faiths, elderly).
2. It is traditional to make turkey with (wreaths, feasts, stuffing) on Thanksgiving.
3. People of all (survive, faiths, harvests) celebrate this holiday.
4. The Pilgrims organized a (feast, wreath, faith) to celebrate that they were alive.
5. Thanksgiving is an (annual, observance, elderly) holiday celebrated by people of all faiths.
6. After the Indians taught the Pilgrims how to plant, they had a good (survival, harvest, wreath).
7. Congress decided to have a day of (annual, survival, observance) for Thanksgiving in 1941.
8. The first year that the Pilgrims were in America many died of (starvation, stuffing, harvest).
9. Thanks to the Indians, the Pilgrims learned to (feast, annual, survive).
10. It is traditional to decorate stores and homes with turkeys, Pilgrims, and (wreaths, stuffing, elderly) of dried flowers and plants.

81

IV. Complete each sentence.

1. The winter in New York can be too cold for old people.

   It can be too cold for the _____.

2. People can die if they do not eat food for a long time.

   They can die of _____.

3. Some people like to prepare tomatoes with tuna and mayonnaise inside them.

   They like _____ in the tomatoes.

4. The flower shop sent a big circle made out of flowers, leaves and a ribbon.

   They sent a _____.

5. The people who got lost in the mountains stayed alive for ten days without food.

   They _____ for ten days.

6. Birthdays are celebrated every year.

   A birthday is an _____ celebration.

7. Many people work on farms to collect fruits and vegetables.

   They come for the _____.

8. The 4th of July is the day to celebrate the independence of the U.S.A.

   The _____ of independence is on July 4th.

9. The family had a big meal to celebrate their reunion.

   They had a _____.

10. You can find people from many different religions in the United States.

    The United States has people of many _____.

V. Ask questions about the sentences below.

1. People of all faiths celebrate Thanksgiving in November.

   a. Who _____ ?

   b. When _____ ?

   c. What _____ ?

2. The most famous Thanksgiving event in New York City is the Thanksgiving Day Parade. At the end of the parade Santa Claus arrives. People watching the parade feel excited and happy.

   a. What _____ ?

   b. When _____ ?

   c. Who _____ ?

   d. How _____ ?

   e. Which Thanksgiving event _____ ?

3. Charitable organizations send food to the needy and elderly.

   a. What kind _____ ?

   b. What _____ ?

   c. To whom _____ ?

4. Thanksgiving was proclaimed a national day of observance by Congress in 1941.

   a. What _____ ?

   b. When _____ ?

   c. By whom _____ ?

   d. Which holiday _____ ?

Christmas

Traditions and Customs

Christmas is a religious holiday. It is the day on which Christians celebrate the birth of Jesus Christ. It is a happy holiday. Families come together to **share** their happiness, attend church, and **exchange** gifts. In the days before Christmas, parties are held in schools, offices, factories, and clubs; homes and stores are **crowded** with shoppers.

Cities and towns in the United States **sparkle** with bright lights and decorations. Churches, homes, schools, shops, and streets are decorated with Christmas trees, colored lights, Santa Claus and his reindeer, and nativity scenes showing the **stable** where Jesus Christ was born. Store windows **display** gifts and Christmas scenes. The traditional colors for this holiday are red and green, and the red poinsettia is considered the Christmas flower. On Christmas Eve, the President of the United States turns on the lights of the Christmas tree near the White House and sends his greetings to the nation.

Families prepare for this holiday weeks before. They make special foods. They make and buy gifts. They wrap them with bright paper and ribbons. They choose a tree and then decorate it with **ornaments** and lights. Houses are decorated with wreaths of holly, evergreens, and mistletoe. Many families share memories by following special ethnic Christmas traditions from their country of origin. Christmas cards are sent to friends and relatives. On Christmas Eve, many read the famous poem "A Visit from Saint Nicholas," by Clement Moore. Children hang up stockings to receive gifts from Santa Claus. Schools usually have two weeks of vacation, and some families take vacations together.

People wish each other a "Merry Christmas" during this holiday season. In many states, people look forward to snow (White Christmas). Christmas carols are sung on the radio and in public places during this season. Some of the most famous carols are "Silent Night," "The First Noel," "Joy to the World," and "Jingle

Bells." There are many shows on television called "Christmas Specials." Films like "A Christmas Carol" (by Charles Dickens) and "Miracle on 34th Street" are family **favorites**. Churches, organizations, and newspapers ask for **donations** of money and food for the needy. **Volunteers** from the Salvation Army stand outside stores collecting money for the needy. Hot meals are prepared and served to the poor and homeless. Toys and games are given to children at Christmas parties by somebody dressed as Santa Claus.

Background

The Christmas story comes from the Bible (Luke 2 and Mathew 1-2). Luke tells a beautiful story of shepherds who were watching their sheep when an angel appeared to them. He told them that a Savior had been born in Bethlehem. The shepherds went there to see Jesus. The baby Jesus was born in a stable. His mother was the Virgin Mary and his father was Joseph. Mathew tells how the Wise Men followed a star until it led them to Jesus. The Wise Men gave Jesus gifts of gold, frankincense and myrrh. Because of this event, the Christians celebrate Christmas.

I. Match words or phrases with similar meanings.

1. **stable** _____
2. **to share** _____
3. **to sparkle** _____
4. **donation** _____
5. **to exchange** _____
6. **ornaments** _____
7. **crowded** _____
8. **volunteer** _____
9. **display** _____
10. **favorite** _____

a. a show; a presentation
b. to give and receive something
c. a gift, an offering
d. something or somebody liked very much, more than others
e. a building for horses and cattle
f. to use or enjoy something with other people
g. to shine, to be brilliant
h. a person who offers to help
i. anything used to adorn, to decorate
j. filled with people

II. Circle the word that best completes the sentence.

1. The movie "Miracle on 34th Street" is a family (favorite, celebration, donation) during this holiday.
2. During Christmas the stores and the streets (display, sparkle, crowd) with lights.
3. It is traditional to buy and (celebrate, volunteer, exchange) gifts with friends and family.
4. According to the Bible, Jesus was born in a (nativity, stable, display).
5. Christmas is a time to (receive, donate, share) the good things you have with others.
6. Many organizations collect (displays, donations, ornaments) for the needy.
7. The stores are so (sparkling, favorite, crowded) during Christmas that it is hard to go shopping.

8. People stop in front of the stores to see the (displays, stables, sparkle) specially prepared for Christmas.
9. Christmas trees are decorated with lights and other (sparkles, displays, ornaments).
10. Many (crowds, needy, volunteers) stand in the street collecting money for the poor.

III. Complete each sentence.

1. The boy gave a piece of his sandwich to his friend.
He _____ the sandwich.
2. The stars were shining in the sky at night.
The stars _____.
3. The merchant gave $500 to the Salvation Army.
He _____ed a large amount of money.
4. The supermarket was full of people; it was hard to go inside.
The store was _____.
5. Manuel liked chocolate cake more than all other cakes.
It was his _____.
6. The family hung all the Christmas cards they received on the window so everybody could see them.
The family _____ the cards.
7. The children bought little toys, bells, and lights to decorate the Christmas tree.
The children bought _____.
8. Many people like to help collect money for the needy. They offer to help during Christmas.
They are _____.
9. Horses eat and sleep in special buildings for animals.
They eat in the _____.
10. During Christmas, people give gifts, and they receive gifts also.
They _____ gifts.

88

IV. Complete the sentences.

1. In a small store, it is difficult to have everything on
   _____ so people can see it.
2. At night all the animals are brought into the
   _____.
3. The skirt was small, so the woman went to the store to
   _____ it for another one.
4. It is better to go to the bank in the morning because at
   lunchtime it is too _____ and you have to wait
   too long.

5. Edward gave Mary red roses for her birthday because they were her _____.

6. Everybody at the picnic put the food on a big table to _____ it with others.

7. The house was _____ because all the lights were on for the party.

8. The sign said, "_____ for the needy will be gratefully accepted."

9. The father went to buy the _____ to decorate the house for the birthday party.

10. There are many _____ helping to collect money for charity.

V. Ask the questions about each sentence.

1. The horses are put in the stable at night so they will be safe.
   a. Where _____ ?
   b. Why _____ ?
   c. When _____ ?

2. During the Christmas holiday, the streets are crowded with people shopping and looking at the stores' displays.
   a. When _____ ?
   b. Who _____ ?
   c. Whose _____ ?

3. People celebrate Christmas by going to church and getting together with relatives and friends to exchange cards and gifts.
   a. How _____ ?
   b. Why _____ ?
   c. With whom _____ ?
   d. What _____ ?

Traditions and Customs

In the United States most people celebrate their birthdays on the day of the month they were born.

Birthdays are celebrated with family and friends. **Invitations** are sent for a party. A birthday cake with candles is served. The number of candles **represents** the age of the birthday person. The candles are lighted. The person makes three **wishes** and then blows the candles out in one breath so the wishes will come true. People sing "Happy Birthday" and wish the person health and long life.

It is **traditional** to bring or send birthday cards and gifts to the birthday person. Many people send flowers. Other gifts can be clothing, books, records, or perfumes. There are birthstones and flowers for each month of the year. These can also be **appropriate** gifts.

Parties for children are usually held at home. At children's parties, children wear birthday hats and get **souvenirs** from the birthday child. Sometimes birthdays are celebrated at school in the classroom with classmates. Mothers bring cake, candy, and refreshments for the whole class. Some parties are **catered** at restaurants. They **reserve** a special room for the birthday group and supply the refreshments and decorations.

Some birthdays are special. Girls have a special **celebration** for the sixteenth birthday, called "sweet sixteen." The eighteenth birthday is important because it is the legal voting age. The legal age for driving and drinking alcohol varies with each state.

Some people want to celebrate the birthday of a relative or friend with a "surprise party." They organize the party, but the birthday person does not find out about it. When the person comes to the party everyone shouts "SURPRISE!"

It is nice to remember the birthday of family and friends. One way to show this is by sending birthday cards, making a telephone call, or sending telegrams. Some people make contributions to **charities** in the name of the birthday person.

I. Match words and phrases with similar meanings.

1. **to represent** ____   a. proper, suitable, satisfactory
2. **wish** ____   b. to provide food for a party
3. **appropriate** ____   c. a small remembrance, a memento
4. **to reserve** ____
5. **to cater** ____   d. a message or note asking somebody to attend a party or event.
6. **souvenir** ____
7. **invitation** ____   e. to stand for, symbolize
8. **charity** ____   f. help given to the poor
9. **celebration** ____   g. something that you want
10. **traditional** ____   h. party

   i. to set apart for special use

   j. practices and beliefs that are passed from one generation to another

II. Circle the word that best completes each sentence.

1. The candles on a cake (represent, celebrate, reserve) the age of the person.
2. It is a(n) (celebration, tradition, invitation) to bring birthday cards and a gift to the birthday person.
3. People make three (parties, birthdays, wishes) before they blow out their birthday candles.
4. Each child at a birthday party may get a (souvenir, wish, invitation).
5. Flowers are (catered, represented, appropriate) gifts for a birthday.
6. Many "sweet sixteen" parties are celebrated at (reserve, catering, charity) places.
7. Some restaurants (reserve, celebrate, appropriate) a special room for children.
8. Families have a special (celebration, representation, charity) when a girl is 16 years old.

93

9. People send (charities, invitations, cakes) when they have a special birthday party.

10. Sometimes people give money to a (celebrity, charity, caterer) in the name of the birthday person.

III. Complete the sentences below.

1. His T-shirt says Niagara Falls.

   It is a _____ of Niagara Falls.

2. The birthday girl sent me a note inviting me to her party.

   She sent me an _____.

3. A smiling face means happiness.

   A smile _____ happiness.

4. The birthday party had music, good food, and lots of fun.

   It was a wonderful _____.

5. We gave money to an organization to help the poor.

   We gave money to a _____.

6. Before blowing out the candles, the boy is thinking about three things he wants very much to happen to him.

   He is making three _____.

7. The parents decided to have the "sweet sixteen" birthday in a place that prepares and serves food and organizes parties.

   The party was _____.

8. The record we bought for Nina was a good gift, and she liked it.

   It was _____.

9. The custom of celebrating a birthday with a cake and candles has existed for many generations.

   It is _____.

10. The restaurant keeps a separate room just for private parties.

    They _____ the room.

11. Wendy says to Manny, "Have a wonderful trip!"

    She is _____ him a wonderful trip.

IV. Circle the word that does not belong.

1. celebration   party   festival   work
2. good   inappropriate appropriate   correct
3. symbolize   represent   stand for   celebrate
4. want   wish   forget   desire
5. provide   serve   celebrate   cater
6. reserve   keep   give away   save
7. souvenir   memento   candle   remembrance
8. letter   invitation   party   note
9. unusual   traditional   old   customary
10. assistance   abandon   help   charity

V. Complete the paragraph.

The bride and groom planned their wedding. They visited many _____ halls. They were looking for a large place because they wanted to have a big, fine _____. Finally they found a catering hall that was _____. They _____ the hall for the date of their marriage. They prepared a list of people to invite. Some will _____ the bride's family, and some will be from the groom's family. They wrote and sent the _____. They decided that the bride will wear her grandmother's wedding gown because it is _____ in her family. They prepared everything carefully, and they had a beautiful wedding. Everybody _____ them happiness and health.

Appendix A: *Appropriate Gifts for Holidays*

Americans give gifts at birthdays, wedding anniversaries, and some religious holidays. Gifts are also given at weddings and births and at showers before weddings and births.

Children are given toys, books, and clothes; adults books, music, clothes, and items for the home or office. Wedding gifts are often silver, crystal, china, or items needed for a new home. Flowers and food, particularly candy, are always appropriate for adult birthdays and anniversaries and as hostess gifts from visitors. Some people use the following traditional lists in gift giving.

Birthstones

January — *Garnet*	May — *Emerald*	September — *Sapphire*
February — *Amethyst*	June —*Pearl or Moonstone*	October — *Opal or Tourmaline*
March — *Aquamarine*	July — *Ruby or Star Ruby*	November — *Topaz*
April — *Diamond*	August — *Peridot*	December — *Turquoise*
	or Sardonyx	*or Zircon*

Anniversary Gifts

1st Paper	7th Wool	13th Lace	35th Jade
2nd Cotton	8th Bronze	14th Ivory	40th Ruby
3rd Leather	9th Pottery	15th Crystal	45th Sapphire
4th Linen	10th Tin	20th China	50th Gold
5th Wood	11th Steel	25th Silver	55th Emerald
6th Iron	12th Silk	30th Pearl	60th Diamond

Seasonal Flowers for Gifts

January — *carnation*	August — *rose*
February — *potted bulbs: hyacinth, paper-white narcissus*	September — *gladiolus*
	October — *aster*
March — *daffodil*	November — *chysanthemum*
April — *tulip*	December — *amaryllis*
May — *lily of the valley*	Christmas — *poinsettia*
June — *peony*	*Christmas cactus*
July — *daisy*	Easter — *Easter lily*

Appendix B: *Holiday Songs*

These songs are a small sample of the many folksongs, hymns, spirituals, and popular songs Americans enjoy at holidays. For certain days, many songs are sung; other days — Halloween and Columbus Day, for example — do not have well known traditional songs.

Christmas carols are heard everywhere: "Joy to the World," "I'm Dreaming of a White Christmas," "Rudolph the Red Nosed Reindeer." On St. Patrick's Day, when all Americans become Irish, "My Wild Irish Rose," "When Irish Eyes are Smiling," and "Sweet Rosie O'Grady" are among many old favorites. Patriotic songs like "Yankee Doodle," "It's a Grand Old Flag," "My Country 'Tis of Thee," and "America The Beautiful" are played by bands and sung by choruses on many occasions during the year.

Auld Lang Syne — (*New Year's Eve*)

Should Auld acquaintance be forgot
And never brought to mind
Should Auld acquaintance be forgot
And days of Auld Lang Syne
For Auld Lang Syne my dear
For Auld Lang Syne
We'll take a cup of kindness yet
For Auld Lang Syne

We Shall Overcome (*King's Birthday*)

We shall overcome, We shall overcome,
We shall overcome some day.
Oh deep in my heart I do believe,
We shall overcome some day.
We'll walk hand in hand, (repeat)
We'll walk hand in hand someday.
Oh deep in my heart I do believe,
We shall overcome some day.

He's Got the Whole World in His Hands (*King's Birthday*)

He's got the whole world in his hands (repeat 4 times)

He's got the little bitty babies in his hands (3 times)
He's got the whole world in his hands

He's got you and me brother in his hands (3 times)
He's got the whole world in his hands.

We Gather Together (*Thanksgiving*)

We gather together to ask the Lord's blessing'
He chastens and hastens his will to make known;
The wicked oppressing now cease from distressing,
Sing praises to his name: He forgets not his own.

Beside us to guide us, our God with us joining,
Ordaining, maintaining his kingdom divine;
So from the beginning the fight we were winning;
Thou, Lord, wast at our side, All glory be thine!

We all do extol thee, thou leader triumphant,
And pray that thou still our defender wilt be.
Let thy congregation escape tribulation;
Thy name be ever praised! O Lord, make us free!

Jingle Bells — (*Christmas*)

Dashing through the snow
In a one-horse open sleigh
O're the fields we go
Laughing all the way.
Bells on bobtails ring
Making spirits bright
What fun it is to ride and sing
A sleighing song tonight.

Jingle bells, jingle bells,
Jingle all the way
Oh, what fun it is to ride
In a one-horse open sleigh! (repeat)

Silent Night, Holy Night — (*Christmas*)

Silent night, holy night, All is calm, all is bright
Round yon virgin mother and child. Holy infant so tender and mild,
Sleep in heavenly peace, Sleep in heavenly peace.

Silent night, holy night, Shepherds quake at the sight,
Glories stream from heaven afar, Heavenly hosts sing Alleluia;
Christ the Savior is born! Christ the Savior is born!

Silent night, holy night, Son of God, love's pure light
Radiant beams from thy holy face, With the dawn of redeeming grace,
Jesus, Lord, at thy birth, Jesus, Lord, at thy birth.

98

Appendix C: *Readings for Holidays*

For some holidays there are appropriate readings which help explain the meaning of the day. Poems, great speeches, and religious writings are often read or recited by heart in public. Here are a few important readings often heard on Martin Luther Kings' Birthday, Presidents' Day, Memorial Day, The 4th of July, and Veterans Day.

The Star-Spangled Banner
The National Anthem

Oh, say can you see by the dawn's early light
    What so proudly we hailed at the twilight's last gleaming?
Whose broad stripes and bright stars thru the perilous fight,
    O'er the ramparts we watched were so gallantly streaming?
And the rocket's red glare, the bomb bursting in air,
    Gave proof through the night that our flag was still there.
Oh, say does that star-spangled banner yet wave
    O'er the land of the free and the home of the brave?

Oh! thus be it ever, when freemen shall stand
    Between their loved home and the war's desolation!
Blest with victory and peace, may the heav'n rescued land
    Praise the Power that hath made and preserved us a nation.
Then conquer we must, when our cause it is just,
    And this be our motto: "In God is our trust."
And the star-spangled banner in triumph shall wave
    O'er the land of the free and the home of the brave!

Pledge of Allegiance

I pledge allegiance to the flag of the United States of America and to the republic for which it stands, one nation under God, indivisible, with liberty and justice for all.

The Declaration of Independence, 1776
Thomas Jefferson

When in the Course of human Events, it becomes necessary for one People to dissolve the Political Bands which have connected them with another, and to assume among the Powers of the Earth, the separate and equal Station to which the Laws of Nature and of Nature's God entitle them, a decent Respect to the Opinions of Mankind requires that they should declare the causes which impel them to the Separation.

We hold these Truths to be self-evident, that all Men are created equal, that they are endowed by their Creator with certain unalienable Rights, that among these are Life, Liberty, and the Pursuit of Happiness — That to secure these Rights, Governments are instituted among Men, deriving their just Powers from the Consent of the Governed, that whenever any Form of Government becomes destructive of these Ends, it is the Right of the People to alter or to abolish it, and to institute new Government, laying its Foundation on such Principles, and organizing its Powers in such Form, as to them shall seem most likely to effect their Safety and Happiness. Prudence, indeed, will dictate that Governments long established should not be changed for light and transient Causes; and accordingly all Experience hath shewn, that Mankind are more disposed to suffer, while Evils are sufferable, than to right themselves by abolishing the Forms to which they are accustomed. But when a long Train of Abuses and Usurpations, pursuing invariably the same Object, evinces a Design to reduce them under absolute Despotism, it is their Right, it is their Duty, to throw off such Government, and to provide new Guards for their future Security.

Lincoln's Address at Gettysburg, 1863

Fourscore and seven years ago our fathers brought forth on this continent a new nation, conceived in liberty and dedicated to the proposition that all men are created equal.

Now we are engaged in a great civil war, testing whether that nation or any nation so conceived and so dedicated can long endure. We are met on a great battle field of that war. We have come to dedicate a portion of that field, as a final restingplace for those who here gave their lives that that nation might live. It is altogether fitting and proper that we should do this.

But, in a larger sense, we can not dedicate — we can not consecrate — we can not hallow — this ground. The brave men, living and dead, who struggled here, have consecrated it, far above our poor power to add or detract. The world will little note, nor long remember, what we say here, but it can never forget what they did here. It is for us the living, rather, to be here dedicated to the great task remaining before us — that from these honored dead we take increased devotion to that cause for which they gave the last full measure of devotion — that we here highly resolve that these dead shall not have died in vain — that this nation, under God, shall have a new birth of freedom — and that government of the people, by the people, for the people, shall not perish from the earth.

I Have a Dream:
Martin Luther King Jr.'s Address at the Lincoln Memorial, 1963

Five score years ago, a great American, in whose symbolic shadow we stand, signed the Emancipation Proclamation. This momentous decree came as a great beacon of hope to millions of Negro slaves who had been seared in the flames of withering injustice. It came as a joyous daybreak to end the long night of captivity.

But one hundred years later, we must face the tragic fact that the Negro is still not free. . . .

I say to you today, my friends, that in spite of difficulties and frustrations of the moment I still have a dream. It is a dream deeply rooted in the American dream.

I have a dream that one day this nation will rise up and live out the true meaning of its creed: "We hold these truths to be self-evident; that all men are created equal."

I have a dream that one day on the red hills of Georgia the sons of former slaves and the sons of former slave-owners will be able to sit down together at the table of brotherhood.

I have a dream that one day even the state of Mississippi, a desert state sweltering with the heat of injustice and oppression, will be transformed into an oasis of freedom and justice.

I have a dream that my four little children will one day live in a nation where they will not be judged by the color of their skin but by the content of their character.

I have a dream today.

I have a dream that one day the state of Alabama, whose governor's lips are presently dripping with the words of interposition and nullification, will be transformed into a situation where little black boys and black girls will be able to join hands with little white boys and white girls and walk together as sisters and brothers.

I have a dream today.

I have a dream that one day every valley shall be exalted, every hill and mountain shall be made low, the rough places will be made plains, and the crooked places will be made straight, and the glory of the Lord shall be revealed, and all flesh shall see it together.

This is our hope. This is the faith with which I return to the South. With this faith we will be able to hew out of the mountain of despair a stone of hope. With this faith we will be able to transform the jangling discords of our nation into a beautiful symphony of brotherhood. With this faith we will be able to work together, to pray together, to struggle together, to go to jail together, to stand up for freedom together, knowing that we will be free one day.

This will be the day when all God's children will be able to sing with new meaning:

My country, 'tis of thee,
Sweet land of liberty,
Of thee I sing:
Land where my fathers died,
Land of the pilgrims' pride,
From every mountain-side
Let freedom ring.

And if America is to be a great nation this must become true. So let freedom ring from the prodigious hilltops of New Hampshire. Let freedom ring from the mighty mountains of New York. Let freedom ring from the heightening Alleghenies of Pennsylvania! Let freedom ring from the snowcapped Rockies of Colorado! Let freedom ring from the curvacious peaks of California! But not only that; let freedom ring from Stone Mountain of Georgia! Let Freedom ring from Lookout Mountain of Tennessee! Let freedom ring from every hill and molehill of Mississippi. From every mountainside, let freedom ring.

When we let freedom ring, when we let it ring from every village and every hamlet, from every state and every city, we will be able to speed up that day when all of God's children, black men and white men, Jews and Gentiles, Protestants and Catholics, will be able to join hands and sing in the words of the old Negro spiritual, "Free at last! Free at last! Thank God almighty, we are free at last!"

Appendix D: *Holidays around the world.*

In teaching students about American holidays, it may be effective to post a calendar in the classroom and to discuss holidays both secular and religious as they occur. Interesting cross-cultural discussions will develop if the holidays from the students' home countries are included on the calendar.

Of course, there are a great many local, national, and international holidays which could be included in the following list, but we have limited ourselves to a few representative local and state, religious and secular holidays and to the official National Day of each country in the world. An exception has been made for the U.K. and our neighbors Canada and Mexico. The dates given were those in 1986. In some cases, these dates may vary from year to year.

An excellent source for up-to-date information and background is *Chase's Annual Events*. It is available from Contemporary Books, Inc., 180 North Michigan Avenue, Chicago, Illinois 60601. Other sources we have used are *The Hammond Almanac, The Information Please Almanac,* and *The World Almanac*.

National Days are indicated by ▀. Religious holidays by ✝, ✡, or ☾. Special state or national days are indicated by abbreviations —(Ill) or (Mex).

New Year's Day	Jan. 1	▀ Saint Lucia	Feb 22
▀ Cuba		▀ Brunei	Feb. 23
▀ Haiti		▀ Guyana	
▀ Sudan		▀ Estonia	Feb. 24
▀ Burma	Jan. 4	▀ Kuwait	Feb. 25
✝ Epiphany	Jan. 6	▀ Dominican Republic	Feb. 27
✝ Three King's Day (PR, Mex, etc.)		Leap year	Feb. 29, '88
✝ Eastern Orthodox Christmas	Jan. 7	✝ St. David (Wales)	Mar. 1
Volunteer Fireman Day (NJ)	Jan. 12	▀ Morocco	Mar. 3
Confederate Heroes' Day	Jan. 19	Town Meeting Day (Vt)	Mar. 4
Robert E. Lee's Birthday	Jan. 20	▀ Ghana	Mar. 6
Martin Luther King's Birthday		World Day of Prayer	Mar. 7
Robert Burns' Birthday (Scot)	Jan. 25	Commonwealth Day	
▀ Australia	Jan. 26	(UK, Can, etc.)	Mar. 10
▀ India		Johnny Appleseed Day	Mar. 11
▀ Nauru	Jan. 31	Girl Scout Day	Mar. 12
Black History Month — Starts	Feb. 1	▀ Gabon	
National Freedom Day		▀ Mauritius	
Ground Hog's Day	Feb. 2	✝ St. Patrick's Day	Mar. 17
▀ Sri Lanka	Feb. 4	▀ Ireland	
Constitution Day (Mex)	Feb. 5	Spring — starts	Mar. 20
Benito Juarez Birthday (Mex)		Earth Day	
Accession of Elizabeth II (UK)	Feb. 6	✝ Palm Sunday	Mar. 23
▀ New Zealand		▀ Pakistan	
▀ Grenada	Feb. 7	✡ Purim	Mar. 25
Boy Scouts Day	Feb. 8	▀ Greece	
Chinese New Year	Feb. 9	▀ Bangladesh	Mar. 26
Mardi Gras	Feb. 11	✝ Good Friday	Mar. 28
▀ Iran		✝ Easter	Mar. 30
Lincoln's Birthday	Feb. 12	Seward's Day (Alaska)	Mar. 31
✝ Ash Wednesday		▀ Malta	
St. Valentine's Day	Feb. 14	April Fool's Day	Apr. 1
Susan B. Anthony Day	Feb. 15	▀ Hungary	Apr. 4
▀ Lithuania	Feb. 16	▀ Senegal	
Presidents' Day	Feb. 17	World Health Day	Apr. 7
▀ Gambia	Feb. 18	☾ Lailat al-Miraj	
Washington's Birthday	Feb. 22	Pan American Day	Apr. 14

Jefferson's Birthday	April 14	
Income taxes due	Apr. 15	
■ Denmark	Apr. 16	
■ Kampuchea	Apr. 17	
■ Syria		
■ Zimbabwe	Apr. 18	
Patriots' Day (Battles of Lexington and Concord, Paul Revere's ride, start of Amer. Revolution)	Apr. 19	
■ Sierra Leone		
Queen Elizabeth's Birthday (UK)	Apr. 21	
National Volunteers Week — starts		
♰ St. George's Day (Eng)	Apr. 23	
National Secretaries Day		
♰✡ Passover (Pesach) — starts	Apr. 24	
Arbor Day	Apr. 25	
■ Tanzania	Apr. 26	
Daylight Savings — starts	Apr. 27	
■ Afghanistan		
■ Togo		
Fast Day (NH)	Apr. 28	
■ Japan	Apr. 29	
■ Netherlands	Apr. 30	
May Day (International Labor Day)	May 1	
Law Day		
Lei Day (Hawaii)		
Be Kind to Animals Week—starts	May 4	
Battle of Puebla Day (Mex)	May 5	
Cinco de Mayo		
■ Czechoslavakia	May 9	
☾ Ramadan — starts	May 10	
Confederate Memorial Day		
Mother's Day	May 12	
■ Israel	May 14	
■ Paraguay		
Armed Forces Day	May 17	
■ Norway		
♰ Pentacost — Whit Sunday	May 18	
Victoria Day (Can)	May 19	
■ Cameroon	May 20	
Midsummer Night (Scandinavia)	May 23	
■ Argentina	May 25	
■ Jordan		
Memorial Day (Decoration Day)	May 26	
Memorial Day (traditional)	May 30	
☾ Lailat al-Qadr		
■ South Africa	May 31	
■ Tunisia	June 1	
■ Weston Samoa		
Coronation Day (UK)	June 2	
■ Italy		
■ Tonga	June 4	
■ Seychelles	June 5	
■ Sweden	June 6	
■ Chad	June 7	
Children's Day	June 8	
☾ Id al-Fitr	June 9	
Prince Phillip's Birthday (UK)	June 10	
■ Portugal	June 10	
King Kamehameha Day (Hawaii)	June 11	
■ Philippines	June 12	
✡ Feast of Weeks (Shebuoth)	June 13	
Flag Day	June 14	
■ Queen's Official Birthday (UK)		
Father's Day	June 15	
Bunker Hill Day	June 17	
■ Iceland		
Emancipation Day	June 19	
Summer — starts	June 21	
■ Luxembourg	June 23	
♰ San Juan Day (PR), St. Jean Day (Que)	June 24	
■ Mozambique	June 25	
■ Madagascar	June 26	
■ Djibouti	June 27	
■ Burundi	July 1	
■ Canada		
■ Rwanda		
■ USA: Independence Day	July 4	
■ Cape Verde	July 5	
■ Venezuela		
■ Comoros	July 6	
■ Malawi		
■ Solomon Islands	July 7	
■ Bahamas	July 10	
■ Mongolia	July 11	
■ Kiribati	July 12	
■ Sao Tome and Principe		
■ France	July 14	
■ Iraq	July 17	
■ Colombia	July 10	
■ Belgium	July 21	
■ Poland	July 22	
■ Egypt	July 23	
Simon Bolivar's Birthday	July 24	
■ Liberia	July 26	
■ Maldives		
■ Peru	July 28	
■ Vanuatu	July 30	
■ Switzerland	Aug. 1	
■ Bourkina Fasso	Aug. 4	
■ Jamaica		
■ Bolivia	Aug. 6	
■ Singapore	Aug. 9	
■ Ecuador	Aug. 10	
Ponce DeLeon Day (PR)	Aug. 12	
■ Congo	Aug. 15	
■ Korea, Republic of		
☾ Id al-Hajj	Aug. 16	
■ Indonesia	Aug. 17	
■ Romania	Aug. 23	
■ Uruguay	Aug. 25	
■ Malaysia	Aug. 31	
■ Trinidad and Tobago		
Labor Day	Sept. 1	
■ Libyan Arab Jamahiriya		

103

▪ Viet Nam	Sept. 2	
▪ Qatar	Sept. 3	
☾ Islamic New Year	Sept. 6	
▪ Swaziland		
Grandparents' Day	Sept. 7	
▪ Brazil		
▪ Bulgaria	Sept. 9	
▪ Korea, Democratic People's Republic		
▪ Ethiopia	Sept. 12	
Hispanic Heritage Week — starts	Sept. 14	
☾ Ashura	Sept. 15	
▪ Costa Rica		
▪ El Salvador		
▪ Guatemala		
▪ Honduras		
▪ Nicaragua		
▪ Mexico	Sept. 16	
▪ Papua New Guinea		
Citizenship Day	Sept. 17	
▪ Chile	Sept. 18	
▪ Saint Christopher (St. Kitts) and Nevis	Sept. 19	
World Peace Day	Sept. 21	
☾ Imamat Day		
▪ Belize		
▪ Mali	Sept. 22	
Fall — starts	Sept. 23	
▪ Saudi Arabia		
▪ Guinea-Bissau	Sept. 24	
American Indian Day	Sept. 26	
▪ Yemen		
▪ Botswana	Sept. 30	
▪ Cyprus	Oct. 1	
▪ Nigeria		
▪ People's Republic of China		
▪ Tuvalu		
▪ Guinea	Oct. 2	
✡ Jewish New Year (Rosh Hashanah) — starts	Oct. 4	
▪ Lesotho		
▪ German Democratic Republic	Oct. 7	
Leif Ericson Day	Oct. 9	
▪ Uganda		
▪ Fiji	Oct. 10	
Gen. Pulaski Memorial Day	Oct. 11	
Dia de la Raza (Mex)	Oct. 12	
▪ Equatorial Guinea		
▪ Spain		
Columbus Day	Oct. 13	
Thanksgiving (Can)		
✡ Day of Atonement (Yom Kippur)		
✡ Tabernacles (Succoth) — starts	Oct. 18	
▪ Somalia	Oct. 21	
▪ Holy See	Oct. 22	
United Nations Day	Oct. 24	
▪ Zambia		
Daylight Savings — ends	Oct. 26	
▪ Austria		
▪ Grenadines	Oct. 27	
▪ Saint Vincent and the Grenadines		
▪ Turkey	Oct. 29	
Halloween	Oct. 31	
✝ All Saints' Day	Nov. 1	
▪ Algeria		
▪ Antigua and Barbuda		
▪ Dominica	Nov. 3	
▪ Panama		
Election Day	Nov. 4	
Guy Fawkes Day (UK)	Nov. 5	
▪ Union of Soviet Socialist Republics	Nov. 7, 8	
Remembrance Day (UK)	Nov. 9	
Veterans Day (Armistice Day)	Nov. 11	
Remembrance Day (Can)		
▪ Angola		
Baha'U'Llah Birthday (Baha'i)	Nov. 12	
Prince of Wales' Birthday (UK)	Nov. 14	
Sadie Hawkins Day	Nov. 15	
▪ Latvia	Nov. 18	
▪ Oman		
▪ Monoco	Nov. 19	
Mexican Revolution Day	Nov. 20	
▪ Lebanon	Nov. 22	
Latin America Week — starts	Nov. 23	
▪ Zaire	Nov. 24	
▪ Suriname	Nov. 25	
Thanksgiving Day	Nov. 27	
▪ Mauritania	Nov. 28	
▪ Albania	Nov. 29	
▪ Yugoslavia		
✝ St. Andrew's Day (Scotland)	Nov. 30	
✝ Advent — starts		
▪ Barbados		
▪ Benin		
▪ Central African Republic	Dec. 1	
▪ Laos	Dec. 2	
▪ United Arab Emirates		
▪ Thailand	Dec. 5	
▪ Finland	Dec. 6	
▪ Ivory Coast	Dec. 7	
Human Rights Day	Dec. 10	
Guadalupe Day (Mex)	Dec. 12	
▪ Kenya		
✝ Santa Lucia's Day	Dec. 13	
Bill of Rights Day	Dec. 15	
☾ Prophet Muhammad's Birthday (Mawlid al-Nabi)		
Beethoven's Birthday	Dec. 16	
▪ Bahrain		
▪ Bhutan	Dec. 17	
▪ Niger	Dec. 18	
Winter — starts	Dec. 21	
✝ Christmas Day	Dec. 25	
Boxing Day (UK, Can, etc)	Dec. 26	
✡ Hanukkah — starts	Dec. 27	
▪ Nepal	Dec. 28	

Suggestions
for the Teacher

These readings and exercises can be used in a great variety of ways, adapted and modified as necessary, in order to fit your teaching situation. Some suggestions are outlined below. In general, the readings and their accompanying exercises may be used either for self-study out of class or for group study in class.

For Self-Study. If the students are to use this book for out of class self study only, it would be a good idea to orient the students to the book and how they are to use it. This can be done in the following way.

1. Go through the first reading with the students (See the group study technique for one procedure). You should point out the redundant style of the readings and encourage them to get into the habit of trying to get at the meaning of a word from the context.

2. Go through the exercises with the students. Point out that there is an answer key, but that the last exercise does not always have answers in the key. You can ask the students to submit their written answers to the last exercise to you on a regular basis.

For Group Study. The basic technique and the variations described below can be used for any of the passages. You can also, to vary the procedure, do some of the passages as group study and some as self study.

1. Refer to the table of contents and have the students look at the key words for the passage. Ask them to note which ones they think they know and which ones they're not sure of.

2. Go over the list of key words for pronunciation. You can pronounce the words and simply have the students repeat them or have the students read them aloud.

3. Option A. Have the students read the entire passage silently. Encourage them to try to grasp the meaning from the context.

   Option B. Have the students take turns reading the passage aloud. Note any pronunciation problems and correct them after everybody has read.

   Option C. You read the passage aloud while the students listen. This option can be done twice. First the students listen with their books closed; then when you read it the second time they can follow along in their books.

4. Have the students do the exercises individually. When they have finished you can ask for questions and clarify problems.

5. When the last exercise asks students to use their own words and there are no answers at the back of the book, you can use this exercise as a test by having the students write out their

sentences on a separate sheet of paper and hand them in to you.

6. Students generally enjoy working together in pairs. This can be a useful in-class variation of self-study.

General Suggestions

1. The sequence of readings in this book is not important. It follows the calendar You may want to read about holidays as they occur, or you may want to ask your students to choose readings which interest them.

2. Divide the class into three groups. Each group does only one of the readings. Then each group explains its passage to the other two groups, putting the key words on the board as it explains.

3. Prepare a double set of 3x5 index cards. Each key word is written on two different cards. For each selection there are usually 10 different words. Shuffle the 20 cards well and write the numbers 1-20 on the back. Place all the cards on the floor with only the numbers showing. Then in turns the students try to locate the matching pairs by calling out two numbers (see "Matched Pairs" in *Index Card Games for ESL*, Pro Lingua Associates.)

4. For review, put the key words from several selections on 3x5 index cards. Divide the class into two teams and have a contest to see which

team can use the most words correctly in sentences.

5. Using the list of American, Canadian, Mexican and British holidays and national days from every country in the world (Appendix D), supplement the readings with talks, interviews and discussions on other holidays. Techniques for initiating these activities successfully are given in Nancy Zelman's *Conversation Inspirations for ESL* and Raymond Clark's *Language Teaching Techniques*. Of particular interest when asking students to discuss holidays from their own country is "Country Talks" in Jan Gaston's *Cultural Awareness Teaching Techniques*. All three resources are available from Pro Lingua Associates.

6. Supplement the readings with further cultural exploration:

a. Ask the students to interview Americans and then compare notes. Detailed suggestions for this activity are given in *Cultural Awareness Teaching Techniques*.

b. Use the material appended to this book to teach songs and to provide a focus for discussions.

c. Plan appropriate holiday observances in class or out. The class may participate in school or public ceremonies. Alternatively, plan a party or celebration. Have the students invite friends or give the party for children or for senior-citizens (See "Time Line," *Experiential Language Teaching Techniques*, Michael Jerald, Pro Lingua Associates). Co-host the party with a church or civic group.

d. Discuss food which is traditional for each holiday. Bring in favorite recipes and menus, and use them as the basis for operations in class (See "Operations," *Language Teaching Techniques*, Raymond C. Clark, Pro Lingua Associates). Then, if you are having a party, help the students prepare the holiday foods using your recipes. Eggnog (New Year's Day), cherry pie (Washingtons' Birthday), and Christmas cookies are examples.

Answers

Introductory Reading

I
1. legal
2. superstition
3. celebrate
4. religious
5. calendar
6. commemorates

II
1. superstitious
2. commemorative
3. illegal
4. celebration
5. legally
6. religion

New Year's Day

I
1. j
2. c
3. b
4. g
5. f
6. i
7. h
8. e
9. a
10. d

II
1. crowd
2. elaborate
3. floats
4. ancient
5. achieve
6. goals
7. embrace
8. resolutions
9. prosperity
10. toast

III
crowds
embrace
ancient
toast
resolutions
goals
prosperity
floats
elaborate

IV
1. toast
2. prosperity
3. ancient
4. goal
5. elaborate
6. crowd
7. achieve
8. embrace
9. resolutions
10. floats

Martin Luther King's Birthday

I
1. e
2. j
3. g
4. i
5. h
6. c
7. d
8. b
9. a
10. f

II
1. memorial
2. segregation
3. integrated
4. discrimination
5. assassin
6. spiritual
7. clergyman
8. racial
   rights
9. injustice

III
1. spirituals
2. injustice
3. clergyman
4. segregation
5. memorial
6. rights
7. racial
8. discriminate
9. assassin
10. integrated

IV
1. memorial
2. spiritual
3. racial
4. right
5. segregation

V
1. actor
2. democracy
3. separation
4. fireman
5. justice

VI
1. d
2. h
3. j
4. m
5. k

6. j
7. a
8. b
9. i, c, m, n
10. 1.

11. i
12. i, c
13. m.
14. g
15. i, f

16. e
17. e, k
18. f.
19. c, m

110

Valentine's Day

I	II	III	IV	V
1. b	1. a	1. decorations	1. romance	1. romantic
2. c	2. d	2. romance	2. spouse	2. festive
3. g	3. a	3. affection	3. feelings	3. humor
4. d	4. c	4. celebrate	4. companion	4. decorated
5. i	5. c	5. companions	5. festival	5. affection
6. e	6. c	6. Merchants	6. affection	
7. f	7. b	7. feelings	7. humorous	
8. j	8. c	8. humorous	8. sweetheart	
9. h	9. d	9. festival	9. merchants	
10. a	10. c	10. sweetheart		

VI 1. f 2. d 3. e 4. b 5. a 6. g 7. h
8. c 9. i 10. k 11. l 12. m 13. j

President's Day

I	II	III	IV
1. h	1. c	1. chopped down	1. chopped
2. c	2. d	2. unite	2. united
3. g	3. a	3. ideals	3. conflict
4. e	4. b	4. admitted	4. elected
5. a	5. c	5. elected	5. ideal
6. i	6. a	6. conflict	6. independence
7. b		7. wrongdoing	7. refused
8. j		8. independence	8. admit
9. f		9. elected	9. wrongdoing
10. d		10. unanimously	10. unanimously

Saint Patrick's Day

I	II	III	IV
1. f	1. bystanders	descent	1. celebrities
2. g	2. participate	celebrities	2. legend
3. e	3. convert	bystanders	3. miracle
4. h	4. miracles	participate	4. convert
5. c	5. celebrities	pennants	5. estimated
6. a	6. pennents	estimated	6. bystanders
7. j	7. estimated	captured	7. participate
8. d	8. captured	convert	8. captured
9. b	9. descent	miracles	9. pennant
10. i	10. legend	legend	10. descended

V		VI
1. celebrated	to celebrate	
2. participation	participatory	1. cars
3. estimation	to estimate	2. facts
4. converted	to convert	3. an idea
5. captured	to capture	4. to observe

Mother's Day and Father's Day

I	II	III	IV	V
1. f	1. raise	raise	1. roles	1. to destroy
2. d	2. respect	roles	2. attend	2. to break up
3. i	3. role	respect	3. memories	3. to dislike
4. j	4. establish	attend	4. symbolizes	4. to be absent
5. a	5. value	establish	5. raised	5. to be unrelated
6. e	6. thoughts	symbolize	6. thoughts	6. books
7. b	7. memories	value	7. proclaimed	7. to be silent
8. g	8. attend	thoughts	8. established	8. action
9. h	9. proclaimed	memories	9. respects	9. to ignore
10. c	10. symbolizes	proclaimed	10. valuable	10. group

Memorial Day

I	II	III	IV
1. c	1. d	1. disabled	1. tragedy
2. d	2. c	2. service	2. disabled
3. i	3. b	3. artificial	3. wrecked
4. e	4. f	4. wreck	4. origin
5. g	5. g	5. origin	5. artificial
6. j	6. e	6. tragedy	6. renewal
7. a	7. a	7. needy	7. needy
8. f		8. patriotic	8. benefit
9. h		9. renewal	9. patriotic
10. b		10. benefit	10. service

Independence Day — The 4th of July

I	II	III	IV
1. d	1. declared	1. declared	1. question
2. e	2. obey	2. naturalization	2. nobody
3. f	3. organize	3. rededication	3. alien
4. a	4. independent	4. force	4. forget
5. b	5. sworn in	5. recognized	5. weakness
6. c	6. representation	6. independent	6. closing
7. h	7. naturalization	7. represented	7. disobey
8. i	8. recognized	8. sworn in	8. destroy
9. j	9. rededication	9. obey	9. dependent
10. g	10. force	10. organized	10. disagreed

V

1. representation	5. force	9. naturalization
2. obey	6. rededication	10. sworn
3. organized	7. declared	
4. recognized	8. independent	

Labor Day

I	II	III	IV	V
1. h	1. message	1. message	1. to rent	1. hiring
2. f	2. hire	2. solution	2. to work	2. requiring
3. a	3. competition	3. strike	3. work	3. striking
4. c	4. wages	4. hired	4. to know	4. persuading
5. b	5. solutions	5. wages	5. to ignor	5. competing
6. d	6. minimum	6. persuaded	6. agreement	
7. j	7. persuaded	7. required	7. problem	
8. i	8. strike	8. minimum	8. maximum	
9. e	9. Unions	9. union	9. to know	
10. g		10. competition	10. individual	

Columbus Day

I	II	III	IV	V
1. d	1. financed	convinced	1. d	1. contribution
2. f	2. convinced	finance	2. b	2. encouraging
3. h	3. contributions	expedition	3. d	3. navigate
4. e	4. ties	comforts	4. a	4. finance
5. a	5. crude	contribution	5. d	5. expedition
6. i	6. encouraged	navigate	6. a	6. convinced
7. b	7. route	encouraged	7. a	7. comforts
8. c	8. comforts		8. c	8. route
9. j	9. navigated		9. c	9. ties
10. g	10. expedition		10. a	10. uncomfortable

Halloween

I	II	III	IV	V
1. d	1. carved	1. costume	1. organization	1. carving
2. f	2. characters	2. ghost	2. costume	2. collecting
3. a	3. ghosts	3. trick	3. character	3. trick or treating
4. h	4. scary	4. carve	4. safety	4. scaring
5. b	5. holy	5. characters	5. scary	
6. g	6. costumes	6. evil	6. trick	
7. j	7. tricks	7. holy		
8. i	8. collect	8. collection		
9. e	9. evil	9. scary		
10. c	10. treats	10. treat		

Election Day

I	II	III	IV	V
1. c	1. debate	advertise	1. not decide	1. duty
2. d	2. election	vote	2. poll	2. registration
3. f	3. results	private	3. public	3. privacy
4. g	4. campaign	Election	4. citizen	4. result
5. h	5. candidates	campaignes	5. organization	5. campaign
6. i	6. vote	candidates	6. irresponsibility	6. voted
7. j	7. duty	duty	7. advertisement	7. election
8. b	8. advertise	results	8. keep secret	8. debate
9. a	9. registration			9. candidates
10. e	10. privacy			10. advertise

Veterans Day

I	II	III	IV	V
1. d	1. forget	1. remember	1. missing	1. remember
2. e	2. found	2. serve	2. buried	2. missing
3. a	3. bring out	3. courage	3. enacted	3. bury
4. j	4. deny	4. missing	4. remember	4. dedicated
5. b	5. insult	5. ceremony	5. courage	5. courage
6. c	6. fear	6. observed	6. ceremony	6. enacted
7. h	7. forget	7. buried	7. observed	7. honor
8. i	8. incident	8. dedicated	8. dedicated	8. observe
9. g	9. be uninterested	9. honors	9. serve	9. ceremony
10. f	10. avoid	10. enacted	10. honor	10. serve

Thanksgiving

I	II	III	IV
1. f	1. food	1. elderly	1. elderly
2. h	2. abundance	2. stuffing	2. starvation
3. b	3. weekly	3. faiths	3. stuffing
4. i	4. young	4. feast	4. wreath
5. j	5. planting	5. annual	5. survived
6. c	6. forgetting	6. harvest	6. annual
7. e	7. games	7. observance	7. harvest
8. g	8. die	8. starvation	8. observance
9. a	9. starvation	9. survive	9. feast
10. d	10. reading	10. wreaths	10. faiths

Christmas

I	II	III	IV
1. e	1. favorite	1. shared	1. display
2. f	2. sparkle	2. sparkled	2. stable
3. g	3. exchange	3. donated	3. exchange
4. c	4. stable	4. crowded	4. crowded
5. b	5. share	5. favorite	5. favorite
6. i	6. donations	6. displayed	6. share
7. j	7. crowded	7. ornaments	7. sparkling
8. h	8. displays	8. volunteers	8. Donations
9. a	9. ornaments	9. stable	9. ornaments
10. d	10. volunteers	10. exchange	10. volunteers

Birthdays

I	II	III	IV	V
1. e	1. represent	1. souvenir	work	catering
2. g	2. a tradition	2. invitation	inappropriate	celebration
3. a	3. wishes	3. represents	celebrate	appropriate
4. i	4. souvenir	4. celebration	forget	reserved
5. b	5. appropriate	5. charity	celebrate	represent
6. c	6. catering	6. wishes	give away	invitations
7. d	7. reserve	7. catered	candle	traditional
8. f	8. celebration	8. appropriate	party	wished
9. h	9. initations	9. traditional	unusual	
10. j	10. charity	10. reserve	abandon	
		11. wishing		

HONK!

115

Key Word Index

achieve 5
admit 24
advertise 68
affection 17
ancient 5
annual 78
appropriate 91
artificial 41
assassin 11
attend 36

benefit 41
bury 73
bystander 31

calendar 1
campaign 68
candidate 68
capture 31
carve 63
cater 91
celebrate 1
celebration 91
celebrity 31
ceremony 73
character 63
charity 91
chop 24
clergyman 11
collect 63
comfort 57
commemorate 1
companion 17
competition 52
conflict 25
contribution 57
convert 31
convince 57
costume 63
courage 73
crowd 5
crowded 84
crude 57

debate 68
decorate 17
declare 46
dedicated 73
descent 31
disabled 41

discrimination 11
display 84
donation 84
duty 68

elaborate 5
elderly 78
elect 24
election 68
embrace 5
enact 73
encourage 57
establish 36
evil 63
exchange 84
expedition 57

faith 78
favorite 57
feast 78
feelings 17
festival 17
finance 57
float 5
force 46

goal 5
ghost 63

harvest 78
hire 52
holy 63
honor 73
humorous 17

ideal 24
independence 24
independent 46
injustice 11
integration 11
invitation 91

legal 1
legend 31

memorial 11
memories 36
merchant 17
message 52
minimum 52
miracle 31
missing 73

116

naturalization 46
navigate 57
needy 41

obey 46
observance 78
observe 73
organize 46
origin 41
ornaments 84

participate 31
patriotic 41
pennant 31
persuade 52
privacy 68
proclaim 36
prosperity 5

racial 11
raise 36
recognize 46
rededication 46
refuse 24
registration 68
religious 1
remember 73
renewal 41
represent 91
representation 46
require 52
reserve 91
resolution 5
respect 36
result 68
rights 11
role 36
romance 17
route 57

scary 63
segregate 11
serve 73
service 41
share 84
solution 52
souvenir 91
sparkle 84
spiritual 11
spouse 17
stable 84
starvation 78
strike 52
stuffing 78
superstition 1
survive 78
swear 46
sweethearts 17
symbolize 36

thought 36
ties 57
toast 5
traditional 91
tragedy 41
treat 63
trick 63

unanimously 24
union 52
unite 24

value 36
volunteer 84
vote 68

wages 52
wish 91
wreath 78
wreck 41
wrongdoing 24

117

Bibliography —
Recommended Resources

Corrigan, Adeline. **Holiday Ring**. Niles, Ill: Albert Whitman & Co., 1975

Burnett, Bernice. **The First Book of Holidays**. N.Y.: Franklin Watts, Inc.

Chase, William D. and Helen M. **Chase's Annual Events**: Special Days, Weeks & Months. Chicago: Contemporary Books, Inc.

Del Re, Gerald and Patricia. **The Christmas Almanac**. N.Y.: Doubleday Publishing Co.

Hoff, Carol. **Holidays and History**. Austin, Texas: Steck-Vaughn Co.

Krythe, Maymie R. **All About American Holidays**. N.Y.: Harper & Row, Publishers, Inc.

McGovern, Ann. **The Story of Christopher Columbus**. N.Y.: Harper & Row, Publishers, Inc.

Myers, Robert J. **Celebrations**. N.Y.: Doubleday Publishng, Inc.

Chambers, Wicke; Spring Asher. **The Celebration Book of Great American Traditions**. N.Y.: Harper & Row, PUblishers, Inc., 1983

Other Vocabureaders from Pro Lingua Associates

Potluck: Exploring American Foods and Meals. Raymond C. Clark. PLA, 1985.

Summer Olympic Games: Exploring International Athletic Competition. Raymond C. Clark; Michael Jerald. PLA, 1987.

The Zodiac: Exploring Human Qualities and Characteristics. Mary R. Moore. PLA, 1984.